TRENDS IN AMERICAN ELECTORAL BEHAVIOR
Second Edition

TRENDS
In American Electoral Behavior

SECOND EDITION

BY
DAVID B. HILL
NORMAN R. LUTTBEG
TEXAS A&M UNIVERSITY

F.E. PEACOCK PUBLISHERS, INC.

Copyright ©1983
F.E. Peacock Publishers, Inc.
All rights reserved
Library of Congress Catalog Card No. 83-61557
ISBN No. 0-87581-296-1
Printed in the U.S.A.

To our parents . . . for the perspective

Contents

Preface to the Second Edition

When we wrote the first edition of this text, our goal was to present patterns of change in American electoral behavior and to do so in a manner that could be understood by an undergraduate. At that time many political scientists found ominous warnings in the voting trends of the 1970s as compared to the 1950s. Others, however, found little cause for alarm, largely because they saw little change in the most important elements of electoral behavior. In all candor, we were in the latter group and still are. We are pleased that other political scientists seem less preoccupied in the 1980s with the potentially negative consequences for American politics of changes in electoral behavior. If it has no other benefit, this should be reassuring to the student reader.

In this edition we have the data from the 1980 presidential election, but the contest between Reagan, Carter, and Anderson does complicate our interpretation. Some trends are reversed, some strongly reassert themselves, and some continue unabated. The relationships between trends, however, hold fairly constant. All of this made the task of revising our conclusions somewhat more complicated than we had hoped. Fortunately, our caution in stating conclusions in the first edition saved us from making predictions about the 1980 election which proved erroneous. We hope that we have done the same for the 1984 election. Probably the strongest new conclusion which we reach in this new edition is that the events preceding the election and the particular mix of candidates that are selected to run, taking into account their personal characteristics and issue positions, are enough to reverse a trend or cause it to soar. The business of trying to draw conclusions about change in American electoral behavior will be unsettling as long as the number of our observations remains limited to a mere handful of presidential contests.

We continue in this edition to bring to the attention of the reader some unanswered questions concerning American elections that are too often given superficial coverage in the average American government textbook. We remain confident that the student is better off knowing the tenuous basis of a conclusion about electoral behavior rather than being surprised when what was thought to be "truth" turns out to be incorrect. Therefore, we have continued to discuss the stability versus change controversy in American electoral scholarship. All analyses have been updated through the election of 1980, but some results of the 1982 congressional elections are also included. Once again we are greatly dependent on the Center for Political Studies at the University of Michigan for their National Science Foundation–funded studies of elections.

As is always the case, our efforts are aided by the research of the many other authors cited throughout the text and the sound advice and suggestions offered to us by others—especially those that have used the book in the classroom. Professor Jim Hutter of Iowa State University was especially helpful in this regard by designing a questionnaire to survey the text's users to ascertain what changes needed to be made in the second edition. His efforts provided valuable information, and we thank him. There are others too numerous to mention, but in particular: Professors Bill Browne, James Carlson, Alan Monroe, A. D. Joseph, Harry Blair, Harry Howard, Patrick Cotter, James Penning, Henry Steck, Stephen Craig, Stanley Moore, William Kitchin, Richard Joslyn, and Sister Kathleen Reagan used our questionnaire to give excellent suggestions for revision.

Finally we continue to thank Ted Peacock for his support and friendship.

David B. Hill
Norman R. Luttbeg
College Station, Texas
August, 1983

Preface to the First Edition

The past several years have brought numerous distinguished rejoinders to that venerable classic, *The American Voter* (1960). Each successive update on the American electorate seems to fuel controversy over the magnitude and meaning of change in public opinion and political behavior. One faction of political science seems preoccupied with the task of demonstrating that Americans are increasingly issue oriented and sophisticated about political affairs. Some members of this faction seem committed, furthermore, to establishing links between issue orientation and other changes, like the declines in political trust and voter turnout. Another faction has sought to reaffirm through the years the continuing relevance of *The American Voter* and many of its conclusions regarding electoral behavior. This faction emphasizes that stability rather than change best characterizes the recent political behavior of Americans.

While these quite different perceptions of trends in electoral behavior are readily acknowledged by political scientists, the "stability versus change" debate has infrequently surfaced in textbooks. There are several potential explanations for this. Perhaps some political scientists may be so engrossed in one explanation that they overlook the existence of an alternative interpretation advanced by colleagues. A more probable explanation is that many textbook authors (and their publishers) believe that students cannot entertain alternative explanations of any phenomena. Some authors and publishers believe that students want "the truth" and are not interested in the vagaries of scholarly controversy. We, too, believe that students can be overwhelmed and confused by academic debate in some instances; but, we also believe that today's student can grasp issues and alternatives. The authors and publishers who do not share this perception sadly underestimate student abilities in our opinion. Therefore, because we believe that students can grasp the essentials of the "stability versus change" controversy, and because we believe it would be unfair and misleading to adopt one position to the total exclusion of the alternative perspective, this book fully discusses both views of American electoral behavior. While we are more comfortable with the notion that the electorate has exhibited substantial stability, the change position is fully discussed and documented.

Numerous individuals made contributions to the development of this book. Several colleagues were helpful in the beginning when we first conceived of this project in the course of a graduate seminar in Electoral Behavior taught by Professor Luttbeg in Florida State University in 1974. Some of the students in that seminar were Carol Cassel, T. Lane Hurley, and Stanley Freedman. John P. Frendreis was responsible for much of the initial data processing. Susan Hoerlein Hill and Alice Thomas Luttbeg read and commented on the manuscript in various stages of its development, as did several anonymous reviewers. Charlotte Jones, Rita Kirby, and Marjorie Franz did most of the manuscript typing. Funds for this research were provided by Florida State University, Kansas State University, S.U.N.Y.–Stony Brook, and Texas A&M University. To all these we express our gratitude.

The data analyzed in this book were collected by Louis Harris and Associates, New York, New York and the Survey Research Center/ Center for Political Studies (SRC/CPS) at the University of Michigan. Neither of these organizations, nor the Inter–University Consortium for Political and Social Research which provided the data to the authors, bear any responsibility for the interpretations or analyses presented herein.

Finally, we wish to thank Ted Peacock and his colleagues at F. E. Peacock Publishers for their willingness to publish a textbook which contains a bit of controversy. Their editorial and artistic assistance has also been superlative.

David B. Hill
Norman R. Luttbeg
Texas A&M University

Introduction

In contemporary political research, a recurring theme is change in the American electorate: change from a model of electoral behavior which was formulated by scholars who studied elections of the 1940s and 1950s. The actual extent of change in American electoral behavior, as evidenced in presidential and congressional elections from 1952 to 1982, is reviewed and analyzed in this book. It should prepare you to decide whether stability or change best describes the behavior of the American voter in recent elections.

In the first chapter we introduce certain methodological considerations related to electoral research. We describe the prevailing model of voter behavior drawn from pre–1960s electoral research. Our method of presentation for this model, rather than simply discussing major research findings and theoretical designs, reviews findings and theory within the historical context of their development by electoral researchers. There is a twofold rationale for this. First, the early history of American electoral research is a seldom–told story which we believe scholars as well as students will find interesting and informative. Our second reason stems from our belief that researchers often have personal biases about how the electorate should behave which subtly influence their research designs and interpretations. By applying the historical approach to the electoral research literature, we can more easily identify various schools of thought and thereby gain a more critical and discriminating appreciation for any given scholar's research and theoretical contributions.

In Chapters 2 through 4 we analyze certain topics which have been identified by scholars as evidence of electoral change. Chapter 2 is devoted to an examination of evidence that political parties are on the decline, both as organizations and as determinants of voter choice. In this chapter we critically evaluate the suggestion made by some researchers that issues and candidate images are crucial factors in voters' decisions to reject or ignore their parties' leads.

Chapter 3 is a study of declining political participation in this country. The primary focus is on voting, but other forms of participation are briefly discussed. Factors which influence voter turnout are given considerable attention in this chapter.

Chapter 4 is an exploration of declining political trust by Americans. In addition to documenting this trend, we look at the decline as it affects attitudes toward specific political objects such as leaders and the national, state, and local governments. Group variations in political trust are discussed as well.

At the conclusion of chapters 2 through 4 we have included a *trend assessment*. It is in these sections that we have attempted to say something new about the electorate. Each trend assessment section is devoted to a thorough and systematic exploration of whether these trends are empirically interrelated. Several interrelationships, which we will discuss, have been speculated on; but few attempts have been made to test the validity of such speculation. The rigorous testing of trend interrelationships is a primary goal of the text.

Chapter 5 considers several additional trends at work in American society, such as increased levels of education, which may be exerting some influence on electoral behavior. This final chapter also enumerates our own conclusions about the extent of change in the electorate and its importance.

While we believe stability is more characteristic of the behavior of the American electorate, every effort is made throughout this book to present the research findings of scholars who suggest that there have been far–reaching, fundamental changes in the behavior of the electorate, beginning in the early 1960s. You will soon recognize, however, that substantial controversy surrounds the study of how people behave politically. In several instances, our own conclusions about change are quite different from those of other scholars whose work we discuss. That supposed experts disagree may cause you some dismay. We hope not. We candidly state, though, that the electorate's behavior is elusive, and our research capabilities sometimes seem dwarfed by the magnitude of the questions we seek to answer. The noted political scientist V. O. Key best expressed this sentiment when he lamented that speaking "with precision of public opinion is a task not unlike coming to grips with the Holy Ghost."[1]

NOTE

1. V. O. Key, *Public Opinion and American Democracy* (New York: Alfred A. Knopf, 1961), p. 1.

"Let me know if I start a trend!"

CHAPTER **1**

Studying the
American Electorate

During the past decade political scientists and other election analysts have debated the nature of change in the behavior of American voters. Almost all scholars agree that there has been fundamental change in certain areas of voting behavior. For example, many Americans have become less partisan, less participant, and less trusting during the course of the past two decades. What is unclear, however, and what divides scholars is conflict over the interrelationship of these trends. Furthermore, scholars disagree over the extent of change in the sophistication of the electorate and the relative importance of factors that influence voters' choices of candidates.

This book attempts to introduce students to change in electoral behavior and unresolved issues in electoral research. In order to accomplish this goal each chapter reviews a significant trend in electoral behavior. Each trend is described fully and documented. And in describing each trend we will point out areas of controversy where political science research has provided inconclusive answers to important questions about electoral behavior.

One probable cause of inconclusiveness in electoral research is the relative newness of political science as an empirical academic discipline in the United States. While there have been forty-eight presidential elections in our nation's history, only the nine elections beginning with 1948 have been analyzed with the assistance of national opinion surveys conducted by social scientists. Therefore, we have relatively few cases upon which to base firm conclusions about citizens' opinions and voting habits.

Of course, we can study presidential elections prior to 1948 by analyzing aggregate voting statistics or studying journalistic accounts. Also, we have the results of a few small–scale attitude surveys which were conducted in small communities during national presidential campaigns of the 1940s. Some of the private pollsters were even doing pioneering work in the thirties. But none of these sources provide today's political scientists with data which have the accuracy, depth, or richness required for modern social science research.

POLITICAL RESEARCH: ACADEMIC VS. PRIVATE

The idea that adequate analyses of the electorate can be hindered by a scarcity of scientific opinion studies may be puzzling in view of the plethora of polls taken during the 1976 and 1980 presidential campaigns. Unfortunately, most such polls are of very limited utility to the political scientist. This is because there are some fundamental differences between private polls (like those conducted for newspapers and individual candidates) and academic polls.

Such differences are more subtle than readily apparent. In general, though, private polls are more concerned with determining *what* the public thinks. The emphasis is on substance and content. *Survey research* (the name academics have given to their own polling) has an additional purpose. Political scientists try to understand *why* citizens hold certain attitudes and what *behavior* is likely to follow from certain attitudes.

One of the differences between survey research and private polling can be demonstrated by comparing the questions each uses to measure the party identification or partisanship of persons interviewed. Pollsters generally ask interviewees only whether they are Republican, Democrat, or independent. This approach is adequate for many purposes even though, as Figure 1–1 illustrates, simple party identification questions with small variations in wording can produce substantially different results. For example, Figure 1–1 shows the different results achieved by different polling organizations, all of which surveyed the public during June, 1982. In addition to producing results which may be unreliable, pollsters' simple measures of party identification do not help us fully understand the meaning and effect of this complex concept. In order to do this better than the pollsters, survey researchers use more refined

Figure 1-1
Pollsters' Party Identification Questions

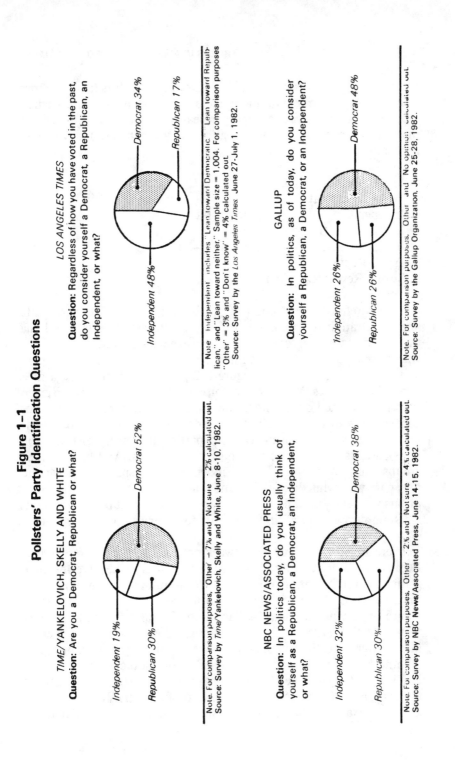

TIME/YANKELOVICH, SKELLY AND WHITE

Question: Are you a Democrat, Republican or what?

Democrat 52%

Independent 19%

Republican 30%

Note: For comparison purposes, Other = 7% and Not sure = 2% calculated out.
Source: Survey by *Time*/Yankelovich, Skelly and White, June 8-10, 1982.

LOS ANGELES TIMES

Question: Regardless of how you have voted in the past, do you consider yourself a Democrat, a Republican, an Independent, or what?

Democrat 34%

Republican 17%

Independent 48%

Note: Independent includes "Lean toward Democratic," "Lean toward Republican," and "Lean toward neither." Sample size = 1,004. For comparison purposes "Other" = 3% and "Don't know" = 4% calculated out.
Source: Survey by the *Los Angeles Times*, June 27-July 1, 1982.

NBC NEWS/ASSOCIATED PRESS

Question: In politics today, do you usually think of yourself as a Republican, a Democrat, an Independent, or what?

Democrat 38%

Independent 32%

Republican 30%

Note: For comparison purposes, Other = 2% and Not sure = 4% calculated out.
Source: Survey by NBC News/Associated Press, June 14-15, 1982.

GALLUP

Question: In politics, as of today, do you consider yourself a Republican, a Democrat, or an Independent?

Democrat 48%

Independent 26%

Republican 26%

Note: For comparison purposes, Other and No opinion calculated out.
Source: Survey by the Gallup Organization, June 25-28, 1982.

measures of partisanship for their studies. Usually this takes the form of discerning intermediate increments or shades of the pure partisan typology. For example, a survey researcher would want to classify interviewees according to the category below which best describes their partisanship:

Strong Democrat (SD)
Weak Democrat (WD)
Independent–leaning Democrat (I–D)
Independent (I)
Independent–leaning Republican (I–R)
Weak Republican (WR)
Strong Republican (SR)

Such careful differentiation of partisanship allows more insightful and penetrating research. For example, political scientists find that there are important differences both between weak and strong identifiers within each party and between independents who lean toward a party and those who do not lean. Figure 1–2 provides illustrations of these sorts of differences. You can see, for example, that strong partisans of both parties stand out as most interested in political campaigns, most concerned with election outcomes, and most likely to vote. On the other hand, weak partisans of both parties are hardly distinct from independents who lean toward one of the parties. And both of these groups stand apart from "pure" independents, especially in whether they care who wins the election and whether they vote. Clearly, much of this subtlety would be lost were we to simply group all Democrats, all Republicans, and all independents together as pollsters frequently do.

There are other differences between pollsters and survey researchers. Because pollsters usually must employ the least expensive means of getting their information, they may cut costs in ways which subtly affect the accuracy of the opinions they seek to assess. One example involves choice of survey participants. The person initially chosen to be interviewed (called a *respondent*) may, for example, not be home when the interviewer visits the home. Pollsters frequently forgo returning to such a home and instead interview a neighbor or another respondent who is at home. The practice of substituting respondents may seriously bias the sample and produce a misleading profile of public opinion. We know, for example, that respondent substitution often results in dispro-

Figure 1–2
Political Attitudes and Behavior by
Partisanship, 1980 Presidential Election

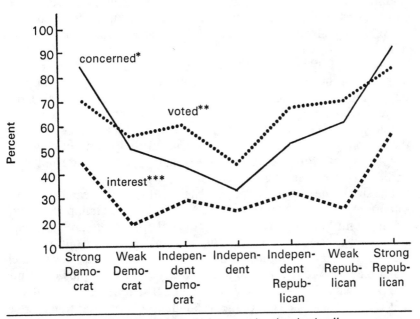

*concerned — "cares a great deal which party wins the election."
**voted — reported voting in 1980 presidential election.
***interest — "very much interested in the political campaigns."
Source: SRC/CPS Election Study, 1980.

portionate numbers of interviews with homemakers and retirees who happen to be home more than family wage earners.

Telephone interviews are another example of the way pollsters cut costs. A typical telephone interview costs 50 to 60 percent less than a home interview; therein lies its attractiveness. But telephone interviewing has two drawbacks which make it generally unacceptable to academic survey researchers. First, the telephone format usually requires that interviews be relatively short, ideally no more than thirty minutes, and limited primarily to closed-end questions. Such questions offer the respondent a fixed choice of responses, and spontaneous or original responses are seldom allowed. This format obviously does not permit the interviewer to go into any depth in following up on interviewees' responses. For example, telephone interviews may show that the public distrusts a particular candidate. But without probing, open–ended, follow-up questions, the telephone interviewer may not find out *why* the candidate evokes low levels of trust. Survey researchers used fixed-choice questions, too; but in respondents' homes, survey research interviewers may spend over an hour with each respondent, probing and following up on key questions often with the benefit of visual aids.

A second problem with telephone interviewing is that it has a built-in bias against the poor.[1] Those who flounder in rural or ghetto poverty often cannot afford the cost of home telephone service. No telephone survey can honestly claim to represent the whole of "public opinion" as long as one segment of the citizenry is systematically excluded from the sampling process. It would be difficult to study non-voting with a telephone poll, for example, because many non-voters do not have phones and could not be interviewed.

The size of the sample used by pollsters and survey researchers is also important. In this area private pollsters like George Gallup made pioneering contributions during the early days of opinion research. Through a long trial–and–error process Gallup determined that the optimal sample size for a national opinion survey is about 1,500 interviews.[2] Such a sample size keeps sampling error to no more than plus or minus (±) 3 percent. This means that if a national sample of 1,500 individuals shows that 25 percent of the respondents oppose additional taxes, then the actual opposition among all Americans lies between 22 and 28 percent. Thus the researcher can be reasonably confident that a 1,500–person sample closely reflects what would be true of the entire population.

Table 1–1 presents the margin of error associated with various sample sizes. These figures are applicable to national surveys as well as samples from smaller populations. Pollsters and survey researchers seldom use samples as large as 4,000 because of the high costs associated with interviewing such a sample. Survey researchers practically never use national surveys smaller than 1,200, but pollsters are increasingly resorting to smaller samples.

The final distinction we will make between pollsters and political scientists has to do with the research style of the two groups. Pollsters generally pay for their research through subscription sales of poll results. Poll subscribers, like newspapers and their readers, are usually interested in election predictions or opinions on a divisive issue, rather than analysis of trends in response to a particular question or the processes of candidate choice or opinion change. Therefore, polls of private pollsters tend to be extremely topical. Questions are dropped once the issue has faded from public interest or rewritten to be germane to the issue as presently discussed, with no concern as to how the rewording complicates the assessment of trends. Political scientists, conversely, emphasize continuity in their research, eschewing the trendy style of pollsters. By using identical survey items over long periods, political scientists can collect survey data which generally allow more sophisticated analyses of change in the electorate.

Table 1–1
Sampling Error Associated with Various Sample Sizes

Number of Interviews	Margin of Error (in percentage points)
4,000	± 2
1,500	± 3
1,000	± 4
750	± 4
600	± 5
400	± 6
200	± 8
100	±11

Note: Based upon sampling error as calculated from experience with the Gallup sample.
Source: C. W. Roll, Jr., and A. H. Cantril, *Polls: Their Use and Misuse in Politics* (New York: Basic Books, 1972), p. 72.

Our discussion of the differences between pollsters and academic survey researchers is not meant to disparage private pollsters. Our only intent is to help you see that pollsters are doing a different kind of research. Pollsters like George Gallup, Louis Harris, and Daniel Yankelovich, among others, have, in fact, made important and lasting contributions to public opinion research. Where appropriate, we will make use of such pollster research. In Chapter 4, for example, we use some of Harris's extensive research findings on political trust in America. But for the most part, the wealth of polls offers little aid in efforts to understand the political involvement of citizens.

LANDMARKS IN ELECTORAL RESEARCH

One book stands at the fore of past academic research into electoral behavior: *The American Voter,* by Angus Campbell and his associates at the University of Michigan. This book was published in 1960 as a definitive study of the presidential elections of 1952 and 1956.[3] To date, over 100,000 copies of this classic volume have been sold.

The American Voter stands as the major landmark in electoral research for two reasons. First, the research techniques used and the questions asked by Campbell and his associates have been adopted widely in subsequent research. Second, the substantive findings serve as the standard against which new research must be judged. Thus, when we speak about change in the electorate, we are generally talking about movement away from the model of voting behavior postulated in this early volume.

Because of the pivotal importance of *The American Voter,* it will serve as the dividing point of our chronological review of the electoral research literature. First, we will review the findings of studies at Columbia University which predate *The American Voter.* Then we will discuss the American Voter model developed at the University of Michigan and summarize its major contributions. Some of the research which has followed *The American Voter* will be presented as extensions of the model.

The Early Years

Most of the very early voting studies came out of Columbia University. Stuart A. Rice's *Quantitative Methods of Politics,* published in 1928, was the first Columbia contribution.[4] One observer noted that Rice's work was "The first noteworthy attempt to connect quantitative research on voting behavior with more general social science problems, such as the study of social change and the determinants of attitudes."[5]

However, Rice's study was based solely upon aggregate voting statistics. No use was made of opinion surveys, as polling was largely unheard of until the mid-1930s, long after Rice's work.[6] Because of his use of aggregate data, Rice had to make many highly speculative interpretations of his findings as they related to individual attitude formation and change. It was twelve years before anyone at Columbia initiated a study of individuals' political attitudes using survey research.

The People's Choice. The first major surveys directed by Columbia researchers were sponsored by the university's Office of Radio Research. This department was later renamed the Bureau of Applied Social Research as its scope of interest expanded. A sociologist named Paul Lazarsfeld directed the first Columbia efforts, assisted by a group of sociologists which included Bernard Berelson and Hazel Gaudet.

Early in his career Lazarsfeld had developed an interest in theories of individual preference and choice. In particular, he and his colleagues wanted to do research on consumer product preferences and to determine what impact marketing and media (radio) campaigns had upon consumer's choices among competing products. To his despair, Lazarsfeld could not locate a foundation or other philanthropic organization willing to fund this project. This prompted him to redirect his research interests. The fortuitous result was his decision to study the impact of political campaigns on voters' choices among competing candidates. The Rockefeller Foundation and Time, Inc. agreed to fund such a study of the 1940 presidential contest between Franklin D. Roosevelt and Wendell Willkie.[7]

Lazarsfeld chose to carry out his campaign study in Erie County, Ohio, and 600 citizens of that county were selected to participate in the main part of the study. These persons were interviewed by the research team on seven occasions before and immediately following the campaign. The sophisticated panel design was employed so that changes in attitudes and candidate preferences could be followed throughout the campaign. The results of this study were published in 1944 under the title *The People's Choice.*[8]

Lazarsfeld's interest in consumer choice shows through in his research design. He hypothesized that campaigns were successful in "selling" products—the products being candidates for the presidency. He felt that if a candidate were properly marketed by the media and other campaign events, much as a new shampoo or toothpaste is advertised, then the public (voters) might purchase (vote for) the candidate.

This consumer preference model of electoral behavior proved to be a disappointment. It was discovered that most voters possessed certain "product" or "brand" loyalties prior to the campaign. These loyalties served to stymie the effectiveness of the campaign in its efforts to sell the candidates. The loyalties citizens held were to their partisan affiliations. Traditional loyalties to their political party's nominee were so great that most of the residents of Erie County knew whether they would vote for the Democratic incumbent (Roosevelt) or his Republican challenger (Willkie) long before the campaign had run its course. Because of this early commitment to one candidate or the other, the citizens of Erie County exhibited little interest in, or knowledge of, the campaign.

One aspect of the Erie County research proved to be more productive. As sociologists, Lazarsfeld and his associates had routinely asked the 600 persons studied about their social group affiliations and personal background. Three variables proved to be important in predicting voting choice. These were: the individual's religion, social status, and place of residence—rural or urban. It was found that Catholics tended to be Democrats and Protestants, Republicans. Low social status and high social status were associated with the Democrats and Republicans, respectively. Rural citizens were more likely to be Republican and urban dwellers, Democratic. These three factors were combined into an Index of Political Predisposition which proved to be a good predictor of an individual's vote. For example, an individual who was wealthy (high status), Protestant, and a rural resident was very likely to vote Republican.

In analyzing citizens' predispositions, Lazarsfeld found that some individuals had been "cross–pressured."[9] This meant that one factor suggested they should vote Republican while another predicted a Democratic vote. For instance, a Protestant, urban resident was cross–pressured between the Republicanism of the Protestant religion and a Democratic urban living environment. Cross–pressured individuals were among the very last to make up their minds about how they would vote. As they approached election day they took one of two alternative courses of action. Some simply withdrew psychologically from the contest and disavowed all interest in the campaign or voting. Others sought more information with which to make a voting decision. The researchers thought that the media might reach these persons, but it was found that they sought advice from personal friends, work associates, and family more often than from the media. Thus, cross–pressured voters resolved their dilemma by going along with the decision of the majority of others in their immediate environment.

The one provocative question dealt with by the author of *The People's Choice* was what role, if any, the media played in the 1940 campaign in Erie County. They concluded that the media had little, if any, direct effect on rank–and–file party voters.[10] However, Lazarsfeld's research group hypothesized that the media did affect voters through a two–step flow of communication, as diagrammed in Figure 1–3. This

Figure 1–3
The Two–Step Flow of Communication Concept

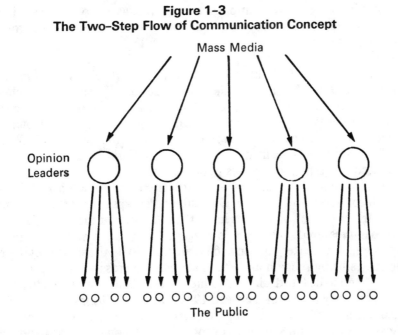

process was premised on the finding that the media campaigns of each party did reach the most highly partisan activists supporting the respective nominees. These strong partisans responded to the media's messages by increasing their partisan commitment. At that point they became *opinion leaders* who tried to mold and shape the opinions of the less partisan citizens around them.

We have gone into fairly substantial detail about this landmark in electoral research. This attention to one early study cannot be said to stem from any particular virtue of the research, however. It may have been fairly exotic for the 1940s, but today it ranks as a rather ordinary project. The importance of *The People's Choice* does not lie in its methodological sophistication, either. A study of attitudes in one county in Ohio could be suspect in its application to voters elsewhere.

Nevertheless, *The People's Choice* remains an intriguing and important study due to the timelessness of many of its conclusions. In the nearly three decades since this study, political scientists have consistently replicated many of its major findings, such as the link between partisanship and secondary group affiliations like religion. They still find that citizens make a voting decision very early in a campaign and that many are not interested in the campaign or any other aspect of politics. Thus this first important study has continuing relevance in the electoral research literature.

Voting. The Columbia research team undertook a second major study in 1948, this time under the direction of senior researcher Bernard R. Berelson, assisted by Lazarsfeld and William N. McPhee. This study was a sophisticated replication of the earlier Erie County, Ohio, project. More persons were surveyed during the campaign (1,000), and the study was located in Elmira, New York. The research was reported in *Voting,* which was published in 1954.[11]

Berelson and his colleagues found little in Elmira, New York, in 1948 which contradicted the earlier Ohio study. Perhaps the most important similarities of the two studies lie in their analyses of the phenomenon of cross-pressured voters. Berelson again found voters who were cross-pressured to vote Republican and Democratic, with the sources of these pressures being religion and social status. The cross-pressured voters were found to be late deciders and more likely than other voters to have changed party affiliation between 1944 and 1948. Elmira was strongly Republican, and this was found to exert enormous influence on cross-pressured voters; most of them eventually went along with the majority in Elmira and voted for Thomas E. Dewey, the Republican nominee for the presidency.

Berelson and his colleagues also made an important observation in Elmira regarding a concept termed *perceptual screening.*[12] Perceptual screening occurs when a voter holds a distorted perception of a candidate's or party's position on some issue. This misperception is not intentional; it is instead a subconscious act by which the voter brings about agreement between his own opinion and his perception of a candidate's opinion. For example, as shown in Figure 1–4, Republicans who favored the Taft–Hartley Act were more likely to believe that Governor Dewey was in favor of the act than were Republicans who opposed the act. (Dewey, in fact, opposed the act.) Republican supporters of Taft–Hartley obviously misperceived Dewey's position. Many Democrats supporting Taft–Hartley misperceived their nominee's position on the issue, too. Harry Truman had vetoed Taft–Hartley in 1947 and campaigned against it in 1948. Still, of those Democrats favoring the legislation, 40 percent were of the opinion that Truman favored Taft–Hartley. This type of perceptual screening occurred on other issues, such as price control and public housing, as well.

Figure 1-4

How Voters' Own Stands on the Issues Affect Their Perception of Candidates' Stands

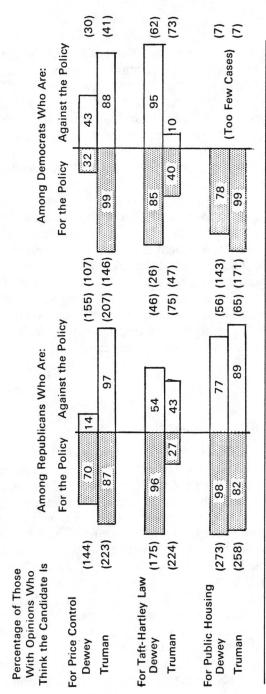

Note: For simplification and clarity, the "No stand" and the "Don't know" responses have been omitted from this chart. The omission does not affect the point of the data.

Source: Bernard R. Berelson, Paul F. Lazarsfeld, and William N. McPhee, *Voting* (Chicago: University of Chicago Press, 1954), p. 221.

Voting also articulated an important theory of political participation. In Elmira, as in Erie County, many citizens were not particularly interested in politics. Neither did they participate in the political life of Elmira. Berelson's commentary on this political apathy was unique and almost without precedent.[13] Rather than condemn political inactivity, as had most democratic theorists prior to the 1940s, Berelson extolled its virtue. He argued that political disinterest and inactivity make a democratic political system more stable and flexible than would be the case with high levels of citizen involvement. He reasoned if everyone in a community like Elmira were to become very active in politics, making demands on the government, then the system would collapse under the pressure of internal political conflict. Needless to say, this rather unconventional endorsement of apathy was controversial. The debate of his ideas which ensued continues today.

Despite the importance of *The People's Choice* and *Voting*, Columbia waned as a center of electoral research. Sociologists at Columbia moved to redirect their research on consumer preference back to projects more clearly related to product marketing and the media. The center of political research moved westward to the campus of the University of Michigan.

Michigan at the Apex: The American Voter Model

During World War II the U.S. government realized that it would be useful to know more about American's attitudes toward various aspects of the war effort. For example, the administrators of the War Bond program needed to know more about why citizens bought and sold bonds. To assist in such opinion research the Department of Agriculture offered the services of their opinion researchers to other governmental units. About this time the Department of Agriculture opinion research unit adopted a new name—Division of Program Surveys.[14]

A list of names of persons employed in the Division of Program Surveys reads like a *Who's Who* in opinion research. After the war, however, many of these noted opinion researchers left government service because of severe budget cuts. Rensis Likert, Angus Campbell, George Katoris, and Leslie Kish left the Division of Program Surveys to establish the Survey Research Center (SRC) at the University of Michigan.[15] The Survey Research Center and its more recently established Center for Political Studies (CPS) have come to be the preeminent electoral research organization in the world.

Since 1948, SRC/CPS has conducted national opinion surveys in conjunction with every presidential election. It also has sponsored (since 1954) a national opinion survey prior to congressional elections in years between presidential elections. Sampling error associated with these studies is quite small, as better than 1,200 persons are interviewed in each survey. Together, these surveys constitute the single most valuable research data available to scholars of electoral behavior. Since many of the same questions have been used in the surveys throughout the years, these data provide the researcher with an unparalleled view of change in Americans' opinions and attitudes over more than two decades.

Three early books and several articles out of Michigan define what we shall call an "American Voter model." The core volume, entitled *The American Voter,* was published in 1960. It was preceded in 1954 by *The Voter Decides* and followed in 1966 by *Elections and the Political Order,* an anthology of essays and scholarly articles.[16]

These books differed from the Columbia research in their approach to understanding political attitudes. This difference was explained through a concept called the *funnel of causality.* Richard G. Niemi and Herbert F. Weisberg have summarized this concept, illustrated in Figure 1-5, as follows:

> The phenomenon to be explained—voting—is at the tip of the funnel. But it depends on many factors that occur earlier. The funnel's axis is time. Events follow one another, converging in a series of causal chains and moving from the mouth to the stem of the funnel. Thus a multitude of causes narrow into the voting act. At the mouth of the funnel are sociological background characteristics (ethnicity, race, region, religion, and the like), social status characteristics (education, occupation, class), and parental characteristics (class, partisanship). All affect the person's choice of party identification, the next item in the funnel. Party identification in turn influences the person's evaluation of the candidates and the issues, which takes us further into the funnel. Then ... (come) incidents of the campaign itself ... Even closer to the tip are the conversations which the voter has with family and friends about the election. Then comes the vote itself.[17]

Michigan researchers concentrated, then and now, on those variables that are closest to the voting decision. This approach can be attributed to the influence of social psychology on modern political science. Today's

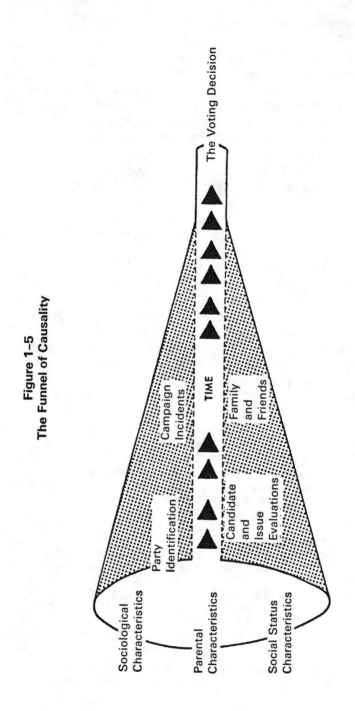

Figure 1-5
The Funnel of Causality

typical political scientist believes that "the immediate determinants of an individual's behavior lie more clearly in his attitudes and his perceptual organization of his environment than in either his social position or other 'objective' situational factors."[18] This perspective is distinctly different from that of the Columbia sociologists Lazarsfeld and Berelson. They, like others of their discipline, dealt with sociological or group variables in the main, variables which are further back in the funnel, away from the immediate voting decision. The perspective of political science does not preclude, however, a continuing interest in the phenomena of group–based political behavior.

Findings and Interpretations.   Several interesting findings and interpretations were advanced by Michigan researchers. We will concentrate on findings of *The American Voter,* the study of the 1952 and 1956 elections. But where appropriate we will discuss later findings which elaborate on *The American Voter* and complete certain elements of the American Voter model.

The fundamental and most repeated finding of this model relates to the importance of political parties in shaping electoral behavior. Simply stated, it was found that most Americans voted for their own party's candidates. In 1952, for example, 99 percent of those who were Strong Republicans voted for Dwight Eisenhower, the GOP nominee, and 84 percent of the Strong Democrats voted for Adlai Stevenson, the losing Democratic nominee. Overall, 78 percent of all voters in 1952 supported the presidential candidate of the party with which they identified. The figure in 1956 was 83 percent.

Thus it is obvious that 22 percent of those identifying with a political party in 1952, and 17 percent of those doing so in 1956, "defected" or voted for the opposition political party's candidate for president. Similar patterns have been found in succeeding election studies. The greatest variance from the party identification and vote relationship has been found in Democrats' support for their nominee. Democrats, through the years, have not supported their nominee with the consistency that characterizes Republican support for their nominee. Nevertheless, partisan loyalty has been the norm in both parties.

The partisan voting finding led to Philip Converse's articulation of a *normal vote* concept.[19] This concept argues that partisan attachment is the prevailing *long–term force* in voting. In elections which are characterized by party voting in the main, the result is a normal vote. But, as Converse and others have noted, all elections are not marked by strong party loyalty. In such elections *short-term forces* prevail over partisanship and cause a deviation from the normal vote. The short-term forces most discussed in the literature are candidate images and issue orientations of voters. (These will be discussed in this and later chapters.)

The normal vote concept has become the basis for a classification of presidential elections as *maintaining* elections, *deviating* elections, and *realigning* elections.[20] A maintaining election is defined as one in which the normal vote is maintained and therefore the majority party captures the presidency. An example of a maintaining election is 1976, the year the Democratic (and majority) party nominated and elected President Jimmy Carter.

A deviating election occurs when short-term forces cause many majority party voters to support the minority party's nominee. This defection to the minority party by voters does not mean they will identify permanently with the minority party, however. The years 1968, 1972, and 1980 are prime examples of deviating elections. On these occasions enough Democrats voted for Republicans Richard Nixon and Ronald Reagan to thwart the normal vote and the maintaining election classification. Furthermore, it should be noted that the victories for the GOP did *not* swing the majority of Americans toward a permanent identification with the Republican Party.

Had Nixon and Reagan been successful in converting more Democrats or new voters to Republicanism, 1968, 1972, and 1980 would have been realigning elections. Such elections are characterized by a "more or less durable" shift in the underlying pattern of partisanship in the electorate. This massive shift would result in the majority party dropping to minority status while the minority party vaults into power.

There have been no realigning elections since the 1930s. The Democrats have maintained their majority status throughout the period following Franklin D. Roosevelt's formation of the New Deal coalition of blacks, Southerners, the working classes, and intellectuals. Some political scientists have speculated in recent years that a realigning election is imminent. Such speculation has two foundations. First, many political scientists have concluded that party fortunes are cyclical in nature. That is to say, a new party gains majority status on a semiregular basis—perhaps every thirty or forty years. Thus, some feel the Republicans' time is overdue and will come eventually. A second reason for expecting realignment is the argument that conservative Southerners will sooner or later leave the liberal Democratic Party. The successes of Goldwater, Nixon, and Reagan in the South in 1964, 1968, 1972, and 1980 were interpreted by many as evidence of impending realignment. But Jimmy Carter's sweeping Democratic victory in the South in 1976 hints that Republicans will have to wait to get the South firmly into the Republican column. We will consider realignment and realigning elections in greater detail in Chapter 2.

The authors of *The American Voter* found that partisanship had a significant impact on voting behavior other than choice of candidate. It was discovered that partisanship (Republican or Democratic) stimulates political participation. Independents were generally less likely to participate in electoral politics than either partisan group. In 1952, for example, only 8 percent of Strong Republicans and 24 percent of Strong Democrats failed to vote in the presidential contest. However, 28 percent of those identified as independents failed to cast a presidential ballot. Strong partisans were also found to be more psychologically involved in electoral politics, expressing more interest in the campaign in 1956 and greater concern over the election's outcome. These findings led some early researchers to conclude that independents were not "good" citizens when contrasted with their partisan fellows. This unflattering characterization of independents has not died easily. We will consider such changes among independents in Chapter 2.

While strong partisans were found to be more involved than independents, neither group was overly active in the campaign itself. Ten percent or fewer of citizens were actively involved in any phase of the 1952 and 1956 campaigns. For example, only 3 percent of the public reported doing any work for either a party or a candidate in those years.[21] The few who were participating were Republicans, by and large.

The American Voter concluded that most citizens restrict their political involvement to the one act of voting. And this act was found to be influenced largely by almost blind allegiance to party affiliation. Thus the voter came to be seen as an uninvolved, dependent creature; this was not the rational citizen that theorists had envisioned populating a democracy.

Probably the most nagging fact relative to this characteristic of how Americans vote for president is that the Republican candidate won both in 1952 and in 1956. In October of 1952, 57 percent of the sample considered themselves Democrats or at least independents who leaned toward the Democratic Party, while only 34 percent were similarly committed to the Republican Party. If party identification is the key determinant of how people vote, Stevenson, the Democrat, should have won overwhelmingly, but Eisenhower was the victor. In 1956, 51 percent versus 37 percent were Democrats, yet Eisenhower won again. Indeed, in presidential elections between 1952 and 1980 the Democrats in the electorate have always outnumbered Republicans, yet Democratic presidential candidates have lost five of eight elections!

Extension of the Model.   Donald Stokes, a coauthor of *The American Voter,* attempted to explain such apparent deviations from the partisan loyalty model. In "Some Dynamic Elements of Contests for the Presidency," Stokes examined data collected between 1952 and 1964 which facilitated comparisons of voters' attitudes toward: (1) the parties and candidates as they relate the domestic and foreign policy; (2) the parties as managers of national affairs and in benefiting groups, such as working men and farmers; and (3) the candidates' personal attributes and style.[22]

Stokes found that the latter attitudes, issue–free opinions about the candidates, fluctuate most from election to election. And he concluded these fluctuations allow the party with the most attractive candidate to win the election. This conclusion does not challenge the notion that most people vote their partisan identification, but it suggests that enough majority party voters desert their party to allow the minority party nominee to be elected on occasion. For example, in 1952 and 1956 Eisenhower got the support of most Republicans and Stevenson got the support of most of the more numerous Democrats, but Ike's personality won him the election by attracting enough disloyal Democrats and independents to claim the victory. Issues, Stokes found, varied little in their impact on these elections and did not determine who won the elections.

Philip E. Converse extended his work from *The American Voter* in an article on the nature of mass belief systems.[23] He found that most Americans do not hold truly meaningful political attitudes and concluded that most individuals' opinions or *belief systems* consist primarily of "nonattitudes." Nonattitudes are defined as attitudes or groups of attitudes which lack consistency, are internally contradictory, and are unstable over time. The implicit conclusion drawn from Converse's work is that most Americans are not equipped to participate in issue–oriented politics. This depiction of an electorate moved by considerations of partisanship and candidate personality, without concern for issues, is perhaps the central concept of the American Voter model.

The crucial nature of partisanship in citizen politics led researchers to study the origins of partisan loyalty. They wanted to know where and from whom people learn their partisan attitudes. The learning of political attitudes such as partisanship is called *political socialization*.

In the 1952 and 1956 surveys, respondents were asked if they could recall the partisan affiliation of their parents. An individual who remembered that both parents were affiliated with the same party was in most instances also affiliated with that party. In 1952, for example, of those persons remembering that both parents were Democrats, 72 percent were Democratic themselves. Only 12 percent had chosen to be Republicans rather than adopting their parents' choice. A similar pattern of transmission of partisan values was found for offspring of Republican parentage.[24]

These early findings of adoption of parents' party identity by children were criticized by some because of the reliance on individuals' recall of their parents' political leanings. Some researchers felt that recall could be unreliable, as those who were interviewed may not have recalled their parents' identification accurately but merely claimed consistency.

Concern about the reliability of recall data led to a second demonstration of parental transmission of partisanship. This more objective socialization study was conducted by M. Kent Jennings and Richard G. Niemi.[25] In a 1965 study they interviewed both children (high school seniors) and their parents. Again, it was found that children adopt the party orientation of their parents. These data, presented in Table 1-2, show that only 7 percent of the high school seniors held a party identification opposite from that of their parents.

Table 1-2
Parent and Child Agreement in Party Identification

Parents	Child		
	Democrat	Independent	Republican
Democrat	33%	13%	4%
Independent	7	13	4	N = 1,852
Republican	3	10	14

Source: M. Kent Jennings and Richard G. Niemi. "The Transmission of Political Values from Parent to Child." *American Political Science Review*, Vol. 62 (March, 1968), p. 173.

The American Voter Model: A Summary. The major points of the American Voter model can be summarized as follows:

1. Partisan identification is the single most important influence in determining political behavior such as voting.
2. Partisan identification is adopted primarily from one's parents at such an early age that personal issue positions cannot be involved in the choice of parties.
3. Politics is not an abiding concern of Americans, resulting in minority participation in most political acts.
4. Given this low concern or salience of politics, few vote on the basis of issues. Partisans largely rely on partisan cues. Less partisan citizens, lacking a disposition to loyally support a political party and its candidates, vote on the basis of personalities or do not bother to vote at all.

This model is controversial, to say the least. As Gerald Pomper observes, "Although the findings are sometimes distorted when retold, the central thrust of these studies is denigrating to the electorate."[26] The ordinary citizen, as described by early Michigan studies, was uninformed, often irrational, and hardly the model of those who assert the value of the common man's role in democratic government.

THE CHANGING AMERICAN VOTER

Some political scientists were dismayed by *The American Voter*—especially its conclusions regarding the apathy and irrationality of the electorate. V. O. Key, one such political scientist, responded to *The American Voter* with a book entitled *The Responsible Electorate*.[27] About this book Key once stated that its "perverse and unorthodox argument . . . is that voters are not fools."[28] Contrary to Michigan researchers, he concluded that American voters were neither "strait-jacketed by social determinants" nor "moved by subconscious urges triggered by devilishly skillful propagandists." He characterized the electorate as being "moved by concern about central and relevant questions of public policy, of governmental performance, and of executive personality."[29]

Key's challenge to *The American Voter* was focused largely on the 1930s and 1940s. Other critiques, based on analysis of change in the electorate since 1960, argue that the findings of *The American Voter* are time bound. These critics point out that the American electorate has changed substantially through the years since the presidential contests of 1952 and 1956. Events like the Cold War, the civil rights and student movements, Vietnam, recession, and Watergate have had a profound effect on the electorate, these critics contend.[30] Some argue that the Eisenhower years of the 1950s were a peculiarly benign time, one in which few political events stirred the electorate. Because of the reticence of the 1950s, some have concluded that it is no wonder that *The American Voter* found such a docile citizenry.

What changes occurred in the 1960s and 1970s in the electorate? Political scientists have claimed three: (1) a decline in partisanship and the role of parties in the electorate; (2) a decline in political participation, especially voting; and, (3) a decline in political trust. We will briefly examine some of the studies which have suggested the existence of these trends in this section, and Chapters 2, 3, and 4 will each examine one trend in considerable detail. We will also consider the proposition that the three trends are somehow related.

Decline of Partisanship and Party

The decline of partisanship is probably the most often cited change in American electoral behavior since 1960. This trend is documented from several perspectives. First, some researchers have found evidence of increases in the number of persons who classify themselves as independents rather than Republicans or Democrats. Also, many other voters who claim to be partisans actually vote as we might expect independents to vote. For example, they frequently vote a split ticket. This split–ticket voting has resulted in an increase in something called *split outcomes*. Split outcomes occur when a state or congressional district votes for the nominee of one party for one high office and a nominee of the other party for another high office. For example, in 1980 voters in the Fourteenth Congressional District of Florida voted overwhelmingly for Ronald Reagan, the GOP presidential nominee; but in the same election these same voters elected a Democratic congressman, Claude Pepper. Substantial split–ticket, nonparty voting must have occurred to cause this split outcome.

A second perspective on the decline in partisanship involves a purported increase in the role of issues and candidate images in voting behavior. Because voters increasingly vote on the basis of these last two factors, they have less need to depend on their partisanship, some researchers have argued. Key, Pomper, and others have made important contributions to the documentation of increases in issue awareness and issue voting. More recent Survey Research Center election studies by Converse, Warren Miller, and others also acknowledge the increasing role of issues and images in voting behavior. There continues to be debate, however, over the actual extent of the decline of partisanship as a determinant of voter behavior, and whether issues or candidate images have replaced party as a determinant.

A third perspective on the decline of partisanship is institutional in nature. Observers of parties as political institutions agree that parties have atrophied. Two causes are cited. First, the decline of party patronage powers has left parties with fewer rewards for loyal party followers, and so some followers have strayed. Second, candidates no longer need or depend on party organizations as in the past. This situation is blamed largely on the communications media. Many observers state that the media allow candidates to approach the masses directly, bypassing the party leadership, unlike candidates in earlier periods.

Decline in Political Participation

The existence of trends in participation depends largely on one's perspective. Since 1960, as Figure 1–6 shows, there has been a 9 percent drop in voter turnout. But 1948's 51 percent turnout may suggest that the early 1960s were abnormally high in turnout. We may now be returning to normalcy. It is also interesting that some observers erroneously predicted that 1976 and 1980 would see presidential election turnouts of less than half of the eligible American electorate. Against this prediction and the seemingly unstoppable decline in turnout, the actual turnout of 54 percent in 1976 and 53 percent in 1980 appear more respectable, especially when one considers that turnout actually increased in a few states. Furthermore, turnout in mid-term congressional elections actually increased in 1982 by a small increment.

In order to place this trend in perspective, it is also useful to note that participation in most other election activities has changed very little. As we will show in Chapter 3, the number of persons working in

Figure 1-6
Voter Turnout for Presidential Elections
Expressed as Percentage
of Voting Age Population, 1948-1980

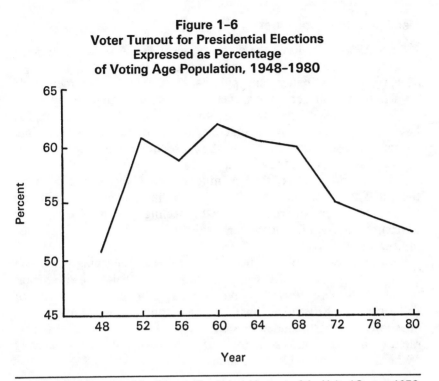

Source: U.S. Bureau of the Census, *Statistical Abstract of the United States: 1978*, Table No. 835, p. 520.

political campaigns or attending political rallies has declined by only one or two percentage points between 1960 and 1980. And only in 1980 did the percentage of persons contributing money to political candidates' campaigns fall off significantly. Thus the decline in voting may not necessarily represent a broader tendency on the part of voters to withdraw from all forms of political participation.

Many political observers are nevertheless greatly concerned about the decline of presidential voter turnout since 1960. If it were to persist, nonvoters would outnumber voters, and the meaning of winning elections might well become obscure to a candidate. As it is, however, only presidential elections, of all elections in the United States, whether at the national, state, or local level, presently enjoy turnouts of greater than 50 percent. So in some respects, presidential elections are given preferential attention by voters even today.

Decline in Political Trust

Since 1960 there has been a steady decline in Americans' trust of government and its leaders. There are two dimensions of this change. The first involves an increasing public sentiment that government leaders are corrupt and serve the special interests. Some might jump to the conclusion that Watergate was the source of such beliefs. Arthur Miller, however, has demonstrated that this trend began before Watergate became a household word.[31] Thus the cause of the decline in trust goes deeper than a Watergate explanation allows.

A second dimension of the declining trust involves *political efficacy*, the belief that the individual has some influence over government. Fewer and fewer Americans have this feeling of control over their government, as studies at the Survey Research Center and Center for Political Studies have revealed.

Such changes in political trust are particularly engaging when one considers that distrust of government was an unheard-of phenomenon in the 1950s. *The American Voter* scarcely mentions the concept of Americans being dissatisfied with their government. In fact, most trust questions were not included in SRC/CPS surveys until the 1960s. This rapidity of change makes the topic of trust perhaps the most engaging of the three trends in electoral change.

THE IMPORTANCE OF ELECTORAL CHANGE

In the preceding section we identified three commonly noted trends in electoral behavior which have occurred since *The American Voter* appeared: declining partisanship, participation, and trust. The importance of these trends lies in their relationship to the stability of our nation.

Theorists and social scientists around the world have long marveled at the stability of American democracy. Except for one major upheaval, the war between the states, American history is unique in its domestic tranquility. No other democracy on earth can match this record.

Most observers of this phenomenon agree that America's stability is not due to fate or simple luck; certain factors have engendered it. The first of these factors is our political party system. It is argued that our two-party system makes for more stable government than would a multiparty arrangement which requires coalitions to achieve a majority. Certainly, two-party countries throughout the world have enjoyed stability, and the United States is a prime example. Multiple-party systems, as in Italy and France, and single-party systems, as in many of the emerging countries, have not been stable.

Furthermore, some of those who question whether government is responsive to the public in this country contend that the two parties usually agree on most of the major issues facing the nation. Disagreements between the parties are seen more in terms of means than ends. These ends are policies which serve the interests of economic and political elites. Because elites and the parties narrow the range of questions open to political debate, they stimulate stability in political affairs.

Political participation also creates stability in America, according to some researchers. Participation, such as voting, is thought to make citizens feel more efficacious, meaning that they can be more confident that their votes do count. Furthermore, by participating citizens are said to gain a sense of being integrated into the political system. Cynics retort that voters are merely coopted by the system; but, as long as participating citizens believe that they are participating meaningfully, the result is a more stable system. A content citizen is not likely to follow the lead of demagogues and revolutionaries.

Finally, political trust is accepted as the foundation of a democratic political system. This implies more than the mere absence of distrust; it means that Americans must actively support, psychologically and otherwise, the political system if it is to persist. While this *systems theory*, promulgated by David Easton, has never been tested, it occupies a central role in American political science.[32]

In summary, the declines in partisanship, participation, and trust have all been linked to the concept of political stability in America. These trends are all in directions which suggest diminished stability. Therein lies their importance. Will they actually bring about increased instability in the electorate? As we examine each trend in the succeeding chapters, we will consider this question

NOTES

1. Charles W. Roll, Jr., and Albert H. Cantril, *Polls: Their Use and Misuse in Politics* (New York: Basic Books, 1972), pp. 96-102; Donald S. Tull and

Gerald S. Albaum, "Bias in Random Digit Dialed Surveys," *Public Opinion Quarterly* 41 (1971): 389–95.

2.   Roll and Cantril, *Polls,* pp. 65–75; Herbert F. Weisberg and Bruce D. Bowen, *An Introduction to Survey Research and Data Analysis* (San Francisco: W. H. Freeman, 1977), pp. 40–41.

3.   Angus Campbell, Philip E. Converse, Warren E. Miller, and Donald E. Stokes, *The American Voter* (Chicago: University of Chicago Press, 1960).

4.   S. A. Rice, *Quantitative Methods in Politics* (New York: Alfred A. Knopf, 1928).

5.   Peter H. Rossi, "Four Landmarks in Voting Research," in *American Voting Behavior,* eds. Eugene Burdick and Arthur J. Brodbeck (New York: Free Press, 1959), p. 7.

6.   Ibid.

7.   Ibid., pp. 15–16.

8.   P. F. Lazarsfeld, B. R. Berelson, and Hazel Gaudet, *The People's Choice* (New York: Duell, Sloan & Pearce, 1944).

9.   Lazarsfeld et al., *People's Choice,* p. 53.

10.   Rossi, "Four Landmarks in Voting Research," p. 19, reports that Lazarsfeld told him in a private interview that this finding was unanticipated by the researchers.

11.   Bernard R. Berelson, Paul F. Lazarsfeld, and William N. McPhee, *Voting* (Chicago: University of Chicago Press, 1954).

12.   Ibid., Chap. 10.

13.   Ibid., Chap. 14.

14.   Richard W. Boyd and Herbert H. Hyman, "Survey Research," in *Handbook of Political Science,* vol. 7, *Strategies of Inquiry,* eds. Fred I. Greenstein and Nelson W. Polsby (Reading, Mass.: Addison–Wesley Publishing Co., 1975), p. 311.

15.   Ibid., p. 312 ff.

16.   Campbell et al., *American Voter,* Angus Campbell, Gerald Gurin, and Warren Miller, *The Voter Decides* (Evanston: Row, Peterson & Co., 1954); Angus Campbell et al., *Elections and the Political Order* (New York: John Wiley & Sons, 1966).

17.   Richard G. Niemi and Herbert F. Weisberg, *Controversies in American Voting Behavior* (San Francisco: W. H. Freeman & Co., 1976), p. 12.

18.   Rossi, "Four Landmarks in Voting Research," p. 37.

19.   Philip E. Converse, "The Concept of a Normal Vote," in *Elections and the Political Order,* eds. Campbell et al., pp. 9–39.

20.   Ibid.; also see Gerald Pomper, *Elections in America* (New York: Dodd, Mead & Co., 1974), pp. 104–11.

21.   Campbell et al., *American Voter,* p. 91.

22.   Donald E. Stokes, "Some Dynamic Elements of Contests for the Presidency," *American Political Science Review,* 60 (March 1966): 19–28.

23. Philip E. Converse, "The Nature of Belief Systems in Mass Publics," in *Ideology and Discontent,* ed. David E. Apter (Glencoe: Free Press, 1964).

24. Campbell et al., *The American Voter,* p. 147.

25. M. Kent Jennings and Richard G. Niemi, "The Transmission of Political Values from Parent to Child," *American Political Science Review* 62 (March 1968): 169–84.

26. Gerald Pomper, *Voters' Choice* (New York: Dodd, Mead & Co., 1975), p. 5.

27. V. O. Key, *The Responsible Electorate* (Cambridge, Mass.: Belknap Press, 1966).

28. Ibid., p. vii.

29. Ibid., pp. 7–8.

30. See especially Pomper, *Voters' Choice;* Warren E. Miller and Teresa E. Levitin, *Leadership and Change: The New Politics and the American Electorate* (Cambridge, Mass.: Winthrop Publishers, 1976).

31. Arthur H. Miller, "Political Issues and Trust in Government," *American Political Science Review* 68 (September 1974): 951–72.

32. David Easton, *A Systems Analysis of Political Life* (New York: John Wiley & Sons, 1965).

VOTE FOR HANLEY

THE DISCO·CONSERVATIVE CANDIDATE

"The old labels just don't seem to mean much anymore."

CHAPTER **2**

The Decline of Party and Partisanship

> The governmental system is not working because the political parties are not working. The parties have been weakened by their failure to adapt to some of the social and technological changes taking place in America. But, even more, they are suffering from simple neglect: neglect by Presidents and public officials but particularly, neglect by the voters.[1]
>
> David Broder

The contribution of political parties and partisanship to American politics is thought to be in a sharp decline. Evidence of this decline has been presented in books and scholarly articles authored by political scientists almost too numerous to count.[2] In fact, none of the other trends discussed in this book can match the decline in partisanship and party vitality with respect to the sheer number of words written about the trend. Political scientists and others have concluded that Americans are increasingly reluctant to identify with the major political parties. Furthermore, partisanship appears to hold less and less sway over many Americans' voting decisions. Paralleling each of these trends has been a decline in Americans' trust and confidence in the political parties and the party system of which they are a part.

INCREASING INDEPENDENCY

The distribution of party identification in the United States from 1952 to 1982 is presented in Table 2-1. The most remarkable figures in this table relate to changes in the numbers of independents and strong partisans. In 1952, only 22 percent of the American electorate claimed to be independent, including those leaning toward one of the two parties. But by late 1982, 30 percent of the American electorate claimed to be independents, down from a high of 37 percent in 1978.

That almost a third of the electorate proclaims independence from parties is balanced by the fact that most self-declared independents willingly admit to leaning toward one of the major political parties. But when we look at those disclaiming any attraction to either party, independents who are not leaning, we still see a substantial change. In 1952 only 5 percent were nonleaning independents, while in 1982 this category had 11 percent, over two times as many.

There is no denying that overall the electorate has experienced a moderate cooling of partisan passions. Scanning across the rows in Table 2-1 indicates the decline of strong partisanship in both parties taken together, from 35 percent in 1952 to only 30 percent in 1982, and the growth of leaners from 17 percent in 1952 to 19 percent in 1982. As the same people were not reinterviewed across the years, these data do not allow us to say for certain that strong partisans have tended to become weak while weak partisans have moved toward independent leaner status. But studies using reinterviews with the same people, called *panel designs,* do measure such partisan movement. In 1972, 1974, and 1976 the SRC/CPS panel shows no such overall movement toward weakened intensity of individual partisanship.

Thus far we have discussed partisanship in only one sense—a psychological attachment to one of the parties. But there are other ways of conceptualizing the notions of partisanship and independency. These involve the behavior of voters. Specifically, there have been marked increases in split-ticket voting and partisan defection in voting. Both of these are accepted generally as symptomatic of increasing independency. We will define these two concepts below and examine some evidence which relates to their existence.

Ticket splitting occurs when a voter casts his or her vote for candidates of two or more parties for different offices in the same election. If enough voters split their ballots, there can be a split outcome for a given congressional district or state. An example of a split outcome is

Table 2-1

Distribution of Party Identification in the United States, 1952–1982

Generally speaking, do you usually think of yourself as a Republican, a Democrat, an Independent, or what? (If Republican or Democrat): Would you call yourself a strong Republican or Democrat or a not very strong Republican or Democrat? (If Independent): Do you think of yourself as closer to the Republican or Democratic Party?

	Oct. 1952	Oct. 1954	Oct. 1956	Oct. 1958	Oct. 1960	Nov. 1962	Oct. 1964	Nov. 1966	Nov. 1968	Nov. 1970	Nov. 1972	Oct. 1974	Nov. 1976	Nov. 1978	Nov. 1980	Nov. 1982
Democrat																
Strong	22%	22%	21%	23%	21%	23%	26%	18%	20%	20%	15%	17%	15%	15%	16%	20%
Weak	25	25	23	24	25	23	25	27	25	23	25	21	25	24	23	24
Independent																
Democratic-leaning	10	9	7	7	8	8	9	9	10	10	11	13	12	14	11	11
Independent	5	7	8	8	8	8	8	12	11	13	13	15	14	14	12	11
Republican-leaning	7	6	8	4	7	6	6	7	9	8	11	9	10	9	12	8
Republican																
Weak	14	14	14	16	13	16	13	15	14	15	13	14	14	13	14	14
Strong	13	13	15	13	14	12	11	10	10	10	10	8	9	8	10	10
Apolitical/ Don't know	4	4	3	5	4	4	2	2	1	1	2	3	1	3	2	2
Total	100%	100%	100%	100%	100%	100%	100%	100%	100%	100%	100%	100%	100%	100%	100%	100%
Number of cases	1,614	1,139	1,772	1,269	3,021	1,289	1,571	1,291	1,553	1,802	2,705	1,211	2,869	2,283	1,408	1,418

Source: SRC/CPS Election Studies. Data for 1952 through 1974 taken from a secondary report on the SRC/CPS partisanship item. See Robert M. Teeter, "Recent Trends in Voting Behavior," in Voters, Primaries, and Parties, eds. Jonathon Moore and Albert C. Pierce (Cambridge, Mass.: Harvard University Institute of Politics, 1976), p. 6. Data analysis for 1976 through 1982 performed by the authors.

when most of a state's citizens vote for the Republican presidential candidate while at the same time electing a Democratic senator and governor. Jack Dennis has reported that split-ticket voting was practiced by only about 5 percent of voters in 1900, but the percentage of split-ticket voters had risen to 32 in 1960. Gallup Poll estimates of split-ticket voting (Gallup asks poll respondents whether they voted for "candidates of different parties") have been erratic in recent elections, but consistently above 50 percent of the electorate: in 1968, 60 percent; 1972, 54 percent; 1976, 56 percent; 1980, 60 percent. The increase in split-ticket voting is evident across a wide variety of elections according to a study by Stephen Shaffer using the SRC/CPS Election Studies. (See Figure 2-1.) Shaffer finds increases in three kinds of ticket splitting between 1952 and 1980: presidential-House; Senate-House and state-local. His analysis indicates that ticket splitting is highest in state-local elections, but the slope of the increase has been roughly the same for all types of electoral races.[3]

A similar trend of increase is evident in split outcomes. Walter DeVries and V. Lance Tarrance studied split outcomes after 1932 in state elections involving simultaneous Senate and gubernatorial contests. They found that split outcomes averaged only 18 percent from 1932 to 1940, with the average increasing to 21 percent between 1952 and 1960. After 1960, some electoral years saw the percentage of split outcomes top 50 percent.[4] More recent data on split outcomes suggests that the incidences of split outcomes may have peaked for the time being, however.[5] As shown in Table 2-2, split outcomes have exceeded 50 percent only once since 1972, averaging about 41 percent since that time. This suggests that, at least in some states, the frequency of split-ticket voting has waned since the 1960s.

Another way to approach the question of increasing independency is through the concept of partisan defection. V. O. Key, Jr., was probably the first political scientist to give systematic attention to the phenomenon of partisan defection. In an analysis of the 1960 presidential campaign, Key implied that psychological identification is not the only or even the best way to identify partisans and independents. Instead Key suggested that independency can be assessed best by examining the voting behavior of citizens.[6] Thus he developed a typology or classification of voting behaviors. The voting electorate was divided into three categories: *standpatters, switchers,* and *new voters.* Standpatters were individuals who voted in the 1960 presidential election for the same party that they had voted for in 1956. Switchers were individuals

who voted for a different party in 1960 than the party they had supported in 1956. New voters were individuals who voted for the first time
in 1960.

Figure 2–1
Ticket Splitting, 1952–1980

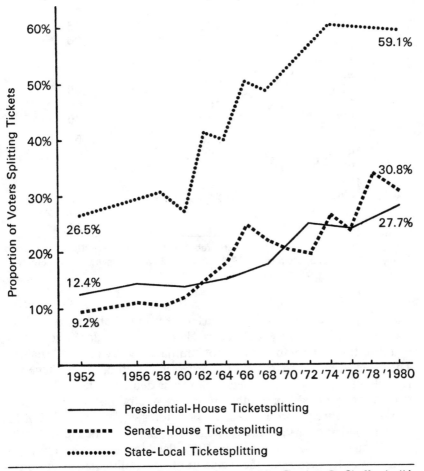

Presidential-House Ticketsplitting

Senate-House Ticketsplitting

State-Local Ticketsplitting

Source: SRC/CPS Election Study data reported by Stephen D. Shaffer in "A
Multivariate Explanation of Rising Ticketsplitting," a paper presented at the annual
meeting of the Southern Political Science Association, 1982.

Table 2-2
Split Outcomes in Gubernatorial and
U.S. Senatorial Elections:
1952-1982

Year	States with Simultaneous Elections	Percent: Split Outcomes
1952	22	27
1954	25	24
1956	20	15
1958	22	18
1960	19	36
1962	27	44
1964	18	56
1966	22	59
1968	15	60
1970	24	46
1972	12	50
1974	25	44
1975	10	30
1976	9	33
1978	24	42
1980	9	67
1982	21	29

Source: Ruth K. Scott and Ronald J. Hrebenar, *Parties in Crisis* (New York: John Wiley & Sons, 1979); data for 1978 through 1982 was compiled by the authors.

Key, as previously mentioned, was quite troubled about some of the conclusions reached in *The American Voter*. In particular he sought to establish that the electorate was not straitjacketed by party allegiance. Therefore, Key was extremely interested in his group of "switchers." He believed that switchers, because of their demonstrated willingness to cross party lines, represented an important strain of independency. In 1960 there were approximately 13 million switchers.[7] While not as great in total numbers as the over 45 million standpatters, the switchers played an important role in the 1960 election. According to Key's study, John Kennedy was the recipient of 10.3 million switcher votes, while his opponent, Richard Nixon, only garnered 2.7 million switcher votes, and this was more than decisive for victory. Angus Campbell and his associates concurred with Key in his finding; their estimates of Kennedy's net gain from switchers was set at 11 percent.[8]

Key's interest in the importance of switchers led him to explore their motivations and issue orientations. It must be remembered that *The American Voter* had typecast independents as ill equipped to wrestle with the complications of politics and voting. However, Key found that switchers, one type of independent, were fairly sophisticated politically. Some of his conclusions were as follows:

> . . . analyses of the available information indicate quite marked corre-
> lations between policy attitudes and vote switching.[9]
> To an astonishing degree . . . voters in their movements to and fro
> across party lines and from an inactive to an active voting status
> behaved as persons who made choices congruent with their policy
> preferences.[10]
> Party switchers move towards the party whose standpatters they
> resemble in their policy views . . .[11]

Thus he began a revision of the notion that independent voters were in some way inferior to their more partisan counterparts.

Subsequent studies by other political scientists have reiterated the theme of increasing political sophistication among independents. Gerald Pomper, for example, finds that independent identifiers are as knowledgeable about government as weak party identifiers, though not as knowledgeable as strong party identifiers.[12] These comparisons are displayed in Table 2-3. We can also see from this table that the level of political activity of independents approaches that of partisans. When there are differences between partisans and independents, it typically is the strong partisan who proves distinctive. But even these differences are slight.

Other researchers have documented the increasing incidence of switching. Walter Dean Burnham, for example, has compared the percentage of votes cast for a party's presidential candidate from one election to the next, using correlational analyses to summarize findings.[13] He calculated a correlation coefficient for each pair of successive elections from the 1940 and 1944 elections to the 1964 and 1968 elections. Extremely high interelection correlations are notable in the 1940s (1940–1944, $r = +0.98$; 1944–1948, $r = +0.96$), indicating an almost total absence of switching by voters between elections. These high correlations did not persist into the 1960s, however. The correlation between

Table 2-3
Strength of Partisanship and Political Awareness, 1972

	Strong Party Identifiers	Weak Party Identifiers	Independents
Accurate Factual Knowledge			
Limit on presidential term	93.1	89.1	89.2
Length of senator's term	43.0	45.0	44.7
Length of congressman's term	59.7	57.7	56.8
House majority party before election	92.5	87.8	87.1
House majority party after election	86.2	84.4	81.5
General Political Activity			
Subjective efficacy	62.6	60.2	57.6
Understand politics	30.0	22.9	27.2
Talk to others about politics	37.1	28.6	31.8
Write to public officials	28.5	24.6	29.9
Vote on all ballot referenda	70.8	69.1	74.4
High general interest in politics	44.9	32.1	36.0

Note: Cell entries are percentages of the given group evidencing the designated behavior.
Source: Gerald M. Pomper, *Voters' Choice* (New York: Dodd, Mead & Co., 1975), p. 33. Data from 1972 SRC/CPS Election Study.

Kennedy's vote in 1960 and Lyndon Johnson's vote in 1964 was only +0.11. The correlation for Johnson's vote in 1964 and Hubert Humphrey's vote in 1968 was +0.23. These correlations should be interpreted with great caution because they attempt to measure individual switching but do so by looking at how districts vote. They do, however, hint that switching, hence voters' independency from their parties, was increasing.[14]

ISSUES AND IMAGES: RISING FORCES IN ELECTORAL BEHAVIOR

The American Voter summarized the forces present in any voting decision as issues, images, and partisanship. The latter was considered the primary determinant in most Americans' voting decisions. Nevertheless, the question of issue voting was given serious thought. The authors of *The American Voter* established three criteria for establishing the viability of issue voting.[15] First, the issue or issues must be known to and understood by the voters. Second, the issue or issues must be salient to (meaning important to or bearing upon) voters. Third, voters must be able to distinguish variant stances by the two parties on the issue or issues. Depending upon the issue involved, between 18 and 36 percent of those surveyed in the 1950s could be considered issue voters in that they satisfied the three criteria cited above.

The American Voter considered the subject of issue voting in one other context. This involved classifying survey respondents according to the sophistication of their political concepts. It was found that, at best, only 15 percent of those surveyed could be called ideologues, the highest level of sophistication about issues.[16] Most voters were found instead to think of politics and issues in simpler terms, such as whether a party favored "their group" or not. For example, farmers would evaluate parties according to group perceptions of whether the parties help farmers. Many other voters simply associated complex political issues or parties with "good times" or, conversely, "bad times." For instance, some voters' positions might hinge on whether they have a good job and income. When times are good, defined by such personal factors as economic prosperity, these voters assume that the incumbent party and its policies are responsible. A third group of voters could provide absolutely no justification or reasoning for its political thinking. This particular attempt to single out issue voters (ideologues) suggested that very few exist in the American electorate.

These findings led to some very controversial conclusions about issue voting in the 1950s. As Stanley Freedman has observed:

> The picture painted by *The American Voter* is not entirely clear. By the criterion of cognition, salience, and perception of party differences, as many as one–third of the voters could be viewed as issue oriented. . . . Yet given low levels of political information and salience, and the fact that party identification acting as a perceptual screen can account for about half of the variation in partisan attitudes, *the usual conclusion drawn from* The American Voter *is that there is a low level of issue voting in presidential elections.*[17]

Since *The American Voter* and the 1950s, most political scientists agree that there have been increases in the roles played by issues and images in voter decision making. The cause and extent of these increases will be considered in this section.

The Changing Political and Social Environment

As noted in the first chapter, *The American Voter* has been criticized as time bound. This is particularly true of its conclusions regarding issue voting. Many researchers have found the 1950s to be a peculiarly issueless period in our nation's history. Consequently, they believe that the findings of the 1950s regarding issue voting hold little relevance for the student of contemporary American electoral behavior.

Several sets of events made the 1960s and 1970s different from the 1950s. Fresh in many Americans' minds was the long and divisive war in Vietnam. This tragic conflict unquestionably served to sharpen many Americans' interest in and knowledge of national issues. But the Vietnam War was only one of many changes in our social and political environment since the 1950s. Social scientists generally agree that these changes must have changed America, including its political behavior. Events or developments frequently associated with political change are enumerated below.

1. *The Vietnam War.* This was perhaps the most unpopular and controversial war in American history. Concern over it led many Americans to participate in protest movements, some involving large-scale violence and civil disruptions. Widespread participation in protests was interpreted by some observers as a new and deep commitment to issue-oriented politics. Violent demonstrators in particular were literally "putting their lives on the line" over the Vietnam War.

2. *The Civil Rights Movement.* Martin Luther King, Jr., wrote from a Birmingham, Alabama, jail in 1963: "Oppressed people cannot remain oppressed forever. The urge for freedom will eventually come. This is what has happened to the American Negro. Something within has reminded him of his birthright of freedom. . . ."[18]

The civil rights movement of the 1960s set many American blacks to thinking about politics, particuarly the politics of equality. Parallel to this new surge in black awareness of the American promise arose the opportunity for full participation by blacks. This was facilitated by the passage of several voting rights acts through which Congress sought to eliminate all barriers to black voter registration, especially in the South.

The civil rights movement also stimulated new political awareness in the white community, as some white Americans sought to protect themselves from integration in public schools and in various facets of business. Concerns of some whites about black activism led to a few unexpected Northern electoral victories by Governor George Wallace in his several campaigns for the Democratic nomination for presidency.

3. *Increasing Levels of Education.*   Philip Converse has pointed out that "perhaps the most massive social change . . . since the 1940s is not itself directly political, but seems calculated to have political effects and is to all intents and purposes, irreversible. This is the rapid increase in levels of formal education of the electorate."[19] Converse notes that in 1952, an election year examined by *The American Voter,* the ratio of voters with a grade–school education to those with any college education was three to one. By the 1968 election, however, college–educated voters outnumbered voters with grade-school educations. It seems reasonable to conclude that this better–educated electorate may be more likely to be issue oriented in its approach to evaluating candidates and making electoral choices.

4. *Increased Leisure Time.*   The rise in education in America has been accompanied by an increase in the living standards of many, if not most, Americans. In particular, Americans have an unprecedented amount of leisure time available for whatever activities they find stimulating. Some observers have advanced the thesis that many Americans have developed an interest in politics in order to fill large blocks of unoccupied time. Politics, therefore, has become a spectator sport, or perhaps even a participant sport for a select few.

5. *Increasing Youthfulness of the Electorate.*   Two factors have contributed to the more youthful appearance being assumed by the electorate. First, a post-World War II "baby boom" resulted in unprecedented numbers of new voters entering the electorate in the late 1960s and early 1970s. Second, a constitutional amendment permitting 18 year olds to vote further enlarged the youth segment of the electorate.

The impact of these changes on issue voting and awareness is not entirely clear. On one hand, young people have traditionally shown a tendency *not* to turn out for elections as well as their elders do. However, young people are also more likely to declare an independent voter status. This status might indicate less reliance on party and a concomitant increase in issue awareness and issue voting.

6. *Increased Influence of the Media.*   The media in general, and

television in particular, are thought by some critics to be exerting enormous influence on public affairs in this country. But while the media have been subjected to considerable criticism in some quarters, political scientists have been, up to this time, extremely slow to take part in such criticism. The most important reason for this lack of criticism is that there have been few studies which establish clear and unequivocal relationships between media usage and the acquisition of particular issue orientations or modes of behavior. Almost all political scientists believe that the media have some influence on political attitudes and behavior, but they are not sure of the actual extent of this influence.

It is reasonable to assert, however, that the advent of the media age ensured soaring media budgets in political campaigns and numerous opportunities for the electorate to witness events happening and to see newsmakers. It is at least plausible, therefore, to believe that this has affected the way people think and vote.

These half dozen developments are likely to have contributed to an increase in the salience of issues to the American public during the 1960s and 1970s. More recently, events such as the deep recession of the early 1980s may have stimulated additional issue concerns among Americans. Furthermore, the greater salience of issues is regarded as being responsible for increases in the incidence of issue voting and the subsequent diminution of party voting. The evidence which has been assembled by various political scientists to document increases in issue voting will be discussed in the following section.

POMPER'S PROPOSITIONS AND
EVIDENCE OF ISSUE VOTING

Gerald Pomper has articulated most clearly the position of political scientists who perceive a rising role for issues in electoral behavior. Pomper's propositions are as follows:

1. In contrast to the past, party loyalty and policy views are significantly related.
2. Over time the parties have come to be seen as different from one another.
3. In contrast to the past, voters show considerable ideological coherence in their attitudes.

4. The effect of issues on the vote has increased considerably, while the effect of partisanship has decreased.[20]

These four theses summarize the important changes that Pomper believes are altering the way most citizens think and feel about political parties, candidates, and issues. Let us examine the evidence that Pomper and others have assembled in support of these contentions.

Party Loyalty and Policy Views

Since their 1956 national opinion–election survey, the University of Michigan's Survey Research Center and Center for Political Studies have asked respondents a number of questions about policy matters. The policy areas involved are: (1) federal aid to education, (2) government-sponsored medical care, (3) government guarantee of employment, (4) federal fair employment and housing practices, (5) school integration, and (6) foreign aid. For each of these areas respondents have been asked whether they favor or do not favor action by the federal government. A respondent who favors federal action is characterized as being more "liberal" on that issue than a respondent who does not favor government action. By comparing responses to these items over time, Pomper has been able to make some important observations.

The first relationship which is evident from these data is that citizens' policy views and their partisan preferences have become increasingly interrelated through the years. Table 2–4 shows that since 1964 there has been a distinct partisan flavor to policy views. Specifically, self-identified Democrats are much more liberal in most of these policy areas than are self-identified Republicans. The only area in which this generalization does not hold is foreign aid. There seems to be no particular partisan bias in favor of the liberal position on this matter. Further examination of Table 2–4 reveals that the relationship between liberalism and Democratic Party identification began in earnest in 1964 and persisted into 1968. However, the relationship appears to diminish in the data for 1972.[21]

Are we to conclude then that the trend toward Democrats being more liberal than Republicans is playing itself out? The answer is almost certainly not. For one thing the way in which the policy questions were

Table 2-4
Party Identification and Policy Position, 1956–1972

Party Identification	Education, Taxation					Medical Care					Job Guarantee				
	1956	1960	1964	1968	1972	1956	1960	1964	1968	1972	1956	1960	1964	1968	1972
Strong Democrat	80.0	66.8	51.0	53.6	52.6	74.2	74.5	78.2	81.3	67.4	75.6	71.2	52.6	53.1	62.6
Weak Democrat	78.1	59.0	44.1	38.3	66.5	67.3	60.2	65.2	72.1	53.1	64.0	62.4	38.4	39.7	44.4
Independent	71.0	53.2	39.3	32.9	55.2	55.8	56.7	57.2	55.3	56.7	55.0	56.6	31.0	27.0	39.5
Weak Republican	68.7	39.1	21.5	22.5	59.3	51.4	47.5	43.5	39.3	36.2	59.5	43.9	25.9	24.9	24.0
Strong Republican	67.7	44.5	15.5	12.0	39.8	45.9	54.2	23.6	42.7	40.9	51.5	52.7	16.1	25.4	20.5

Party Identification	Fair Employment					School Integration					Foreign Aid				
	1956	1960	1964	1968	1972	1956	1960	1964	1968	1972	1956	1960	1964	1968	1972
Strong Democrat	73.3	63.0	56.3	61.9	64.9	38.7	39.8	53.7	58.9	55.3	49.5	51.4	64.7	51.3	38.9
Weak Democrat	71.3	63.1	42.9	43.5	53.0	44.4	37.5	43.2	44.6	43.1	55.4	48.8	59.2	45.8	44.7
Independent	66.6	65.4	50.3	37.7	55.2	48.8	47.1	49.0	37.3	45.6	49.9	53.2	57.5	42.7	47.4
Weak Republican	70.8	62.7	36.3	37.8	51.0	49.3	43.0	50.5	37.4	45.4	48.2	54.0	56.6	47.0	44.0
Strong Republican	66.8	65.9	20.6	31.3	39.4	38.8	41.5	34.8	31.5	34.8	51.4	61.5	49.7	41.8	47.8

Note: The percentage in each cell is that supporting the "liberal" position.
Source: Gerald M. Pomper, *Voters' Choice* (New York: Dodd, Mead & Co., 1975), p. 168. Data from SRC/CPS Election Studies.

asked in 1972 differed from the way they were asked in prior years. This may explain to some extent the 1972 finding. Furthermore, other studies of partisanship and ideology which make use of post-1972 data confirm the continued existence of a linkage between the two. One study has combined the 1973–1977 National Opinion Research Center's (NORC) General Social Surveys and demonstrated that Democrats are more likely to identify themselves as liberals while Republicans classify themselves as conservatives. During the years examined, 60 percent of strong Republicans and 41 percent of weak Republicans labeled themselves "conservative." On the Democratic side, only 23 percent of strong Democrats and 25 percent of weak Democrats labeled themselves conservative. While many Democrats, especially weak identifiers, saw themselves as moderates, a plurality of strong Democrats (about 40 percent) classified themselves as liberal.[22] Therefore it appears that the linkage between partisanship and political views persisted into the 1970s, although perhaps not as strongly as it was in the 1960s.

Party Differences Perceived

Pomper also found in his longitudinal analyses of the SRC/CPS policy questions that the public has become increasingly aware of policy differences between the Democratic and Republican parties. Furthermore, among those persons perceiving differences between the two parties, there has been an increase over time in the percentage of citizens who correctly perceive the parties' differences.

The extent of change detected by Pomper seems impressive. Across the six policy areas, between 1956 and 1968, he found a 9 percent gain in the ranks of those who perceived differences between the parties. Among those persons who perceived a difference, there was a 24 percent upward incremental change in the numbers of persons correctly identifying the Democrats as the "liberal" party on the six issues. Although the 1972 questions were altered from those of previous years (as we have noted), Pomper concluded that "Despite changes in questions and methods, the voters continue [in 1972] to perceive differences between the Democrats and Republicans."[23]

Data taken from Gallup Poll reports are not as supportive of the notion that Americans have more clearly perceived differences, correctly or incorrectly, between the Republicans and the Democrats. In 1960 and again in 1980, Gallup asked a sampling of Americans which political party could best handle the nation's most important problem (which each respondent was asked to identify) and which party would be best for people like themselves. On both questions, as shown in Table 2-5, there has been little change in the percentage of those polled that perceive little or no difference between the two parties. There was, in fact, a very tiny increase in the proportion of persons that saw no difference between the parties in terms of their capacity to handle the most important problems. While these data do nothing to specifically refute Pomper's conclusion that parties were perceived differently by 1972 in their positions on various issues, the Gallup reports do suggest that caution is advised in arriving at strong conclusions about changes in popular conceptions of party differences.

Table 2-5
Perceptions of No Differences in Parties,
1960 and 1980

	Which party is best for people like yourself? (% "no difference")	Which party is best able to handle nation's most important problem? (% "uncommitted")
1960	18	41
1980	14	43

Source: *Gallup Opinion Index,* Report #187 (April, 1981) and Report #194 (November, 1981).

Better Belief Systems

Pomper also has cited a trend toward attitude consistency as evidence of the increasing role of issues in the electorate. Several researchers confirm such a trend, but its magnitude is subject to dispute.

Philip Converse, who has been concerned with the quality of Americans' belief systems, found that most Americans did not have a constrained set of beliefs between 1956 and 1960. Most Americans' beliefs were inconsistent, often internally contradictory, and unstable over time. In fact, Converse found attitude changes among many Americans which appeared almost random in nature.[24]

More recently, Norman Nie and Kristi Anderson claim to have found some improvement in Americans' belief systems. In their analysis of the 1960s and 1970s, they use Converse's general techniques and methods and detected a striking improvement in ideological constraint between 1960 and 1964. This constraint has diminished to a small degree since 1964, but it persists at levels which surpass those noted earlier by Converse. Nie and Anderson also find that levels of ideological consistency have risen more for domestic policy issues than for foreign policy issues.[25]

These findings were supported by the SRC/CPS's analysis of the 1972 presidential election. In that study, Arthur Miller and his associates concluded that high levels of ideological constraint in 1972 were prompted by public reaction to events like Vietnam and racial conflict.[26] Nie notes similarly that "The political events of the last decade, and the crisis atmosphere which has attended them, have caused citizens to perceive politics as increasingly central to their lives."[27] Nie concurs with Miller, furthermore, by concluding that political events stimulated increased attitude consistency in the sixties. He also rejects the thesis that increases in education levels of the electorate can adequately account for the observed changes.

At least three studies have been critical of Nie and Anderson's conclusions about increased ideological consistency, however.[28] Two studies suggest that the Nie finding was simply an artifact of changes in the format of SRC/CPS survey questions. Another study, by Converse and Marcus, examines consistency of issue attitudes across the 1956–60 and 1972–76 panel studies. (In each panel study respondents were interviewed during each of the three election years that fell during the panel.) If N. Nie is correct that ideological consistency is improving, Converse and Marcus reasoned that consistency across the 1972–76 panel study should be greater than that observed across the 1952–56 panel study. But this increase in consistency did not occur on issues that were included in both panel periods. Taken as a whole, these three studies cast serious doubt on Nie's conclusions.

Other related research also fails to support the proposition that Americans are exhibiting greater consistency in opinions on issues such as Medicare, school integration, and foreign aid.[29] Little or no consistency was evident before 1964, as shown in Figure 2-2. Those who favored Medicare were as likely to disapprove of school integration as they were to approve. No consistent pattern was evident of a liberal stance on one issue to another. Some increase in consistency is to be noted by 1968, but this increase is very minimal and it is followed by declines. As is so typical of trends discussed in this chapter, change is evident, but we feel the magnitude of the trend fails to support the optimism of researchers who emphasize the new role of issues in contemporary electoral behavior.

Figure 2-2
Correlations Between Opinions on Medical Insurance, School Integration, and Foreign Aid, 1956-1976

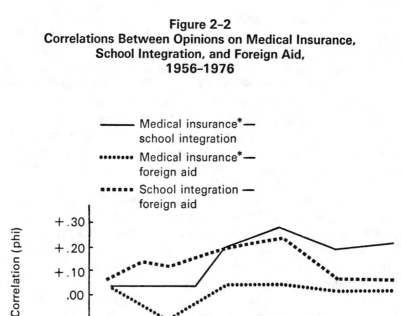

*Question wordings were changed substantially over the years, especially on medical insurance, as the early questions (until 1972) were on Medicare, while those thereafter dealt with medical insurance for everyone.

Source: Data for 1956-1968 from Robert S. Erikson and Norman R. Luttbeg, *American Public Opinion: Its Origins, Content, and Impact* (New York: John Wiley & Sons, 1973). Data for 1972 and 1976 calculated by Norman R. Luttbeg.

Voting: The Link with Issues and Images

Another facet of the rise of issues concerns the increasing connection between issues and voting. The available evidence does suggest that issue voting is definitely on the rise. However, increasing issue voting has been accompanied by another phenomenon—an increase in candidate–image voting. And according to research conducted by Eugene DeClercq, Thomas Hurley, and Norman Luttbeg, the increase in candidate–image voting has outstripped growth in the role of issues.[30]

Candidate image is a term to describe the personal characteristics of a candidate which a voter finds appealing or unappealing. However, these characteristics are unrelated to the candidate's policy or partisan views. The candidate may be viewed as appealing solely because of personal factors such as physical appearance, intelligence, schooling, family background, or speech.

A second image variable employed by DeClercq and his associates is *party image*. This is another evaluation devoid of specific policy concerns. For example, a Kansas wheat farmer may say that he votes Republican because "Republicans are the party of the farmer." In our view, such a response lacks any specific policy content. It is possible, however, that the farmer has observed that the Republican party supports farm policies that he personally favors. Our own belief, nevertheless, is that policy content of this variety is seldom the foundation of party image responses.

The question these authors sought to answer was: What has been the relative impact of four variables on Americans' voting decisions in presidential elections between 1956 and 1972? The four variables considered were (1) candidate image, (2) issue orientation, (3) party identification, and (4) party image. Their findings, updated through 1980, are displayed in Figure 2–3. While the measure used here is somewhat complex, you need only note that a variable with a Beta of 0.4 has twice the impact on how people vote as does one of 0.2.

The trend lines depicted in Figure 2–3 indicate that, with the exception of the 1972 presidential election, party identification has prevailed over the other determinants of voter choice, but only narrowly so in 1980. After the 1972 election and the precipitous drop in the importance of partisanship, there was much discussion to the effect that party identification would no longer dominate voters' decision making. Nevertheless, partisanship reemerged as the most important factor in 1976, only to fall again in 1980. With this perspective of recent elec-

Figure 2–3
Factors Influencing Presidential Voting, 1956–1980
(Betas using average standard deviations across elections)

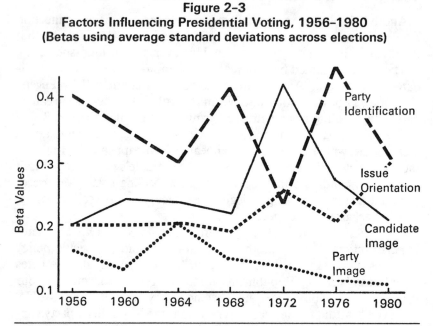

Source: Eugene DeClercq, Thomas L. Hurley, and Norman R. Luttbeg, "Voting in American Presidential Elections," *American Politics Quarterly* 3, no. 3 (July 1975). Analysis updated for 1976 by Thomas L. Hurley; analysis updated for 1980 by Norman R. Luttbeg. Data from SRC/CPS Election Studies.

tions, it is difficult to predict the future importance of party identification or any other of the four factors analyzed, other than to say that issues are slowly and consistently rising in importance over time. It seems likely that the erratic performance of these factors over the last four elections will continue as we enter an era of dynamic electoral behavior in which the absolute and relative effects of partisanship, issues, and images will fluctuate.

THE SHRINKING ROLE OF PARTIES AS ORGANIZATIONS

Antiparty sentiment has always been a dynamic element of American politics. Joyce Gelb and Marian Lief Palley have very clearly defined the term *antiparty politics* as a:

... negative response—almost a fear—Americans have toward political parties. It refers to a general unwillingness to participate in party
activities or to provide parties with any greater authority or responsibility than is absolutely necessary to nominate and elect candidates
to public elective office or to perform as agents of policymaking.[31]

This antipathy for parties was widely shared by our Founding Fathers. James Madison, for example, wrote that the primary function of government was to control those forces within society that
seek to divide men and women into groups or factions. There can
be little doubt that Madison and his colleagues initially opposed the
idea of establishing parties because of the divisiveness that parties
would represent. But as time passed leaders like Madison recognized that abolition of parties was not a reasonable goal. Instead,
their attention was redirected to controlling the effects of parties and
other factions.

Elite theorists argue that the result of the Founding Fathers' redirec-
tion was the establishment of a two-party system in which there is
relatively little difference in party ideologies. And, as we observed
earlier in this chapter, even today the American people often have
difficulty distinguishing between the two parties. Critics of American
democracy and its parties argue that the lack of ideological distinctive-
ness in our party system serves the interests of the status quo in public
policy.

In conclusion, the Founding Fathers created, and others have perpet-
uated, a party system which narrows the range of political choices
offered to the citizenry. This narrowing of choices has sometimes been
credited with enhancing the public's dim view of parties. But as you will
see, this is not the only criticism directed toward the parties and the
party system; politicians have joined the public in rebelling against the
parties as electoral organizations.

Loss of Patronage Powers

Because of their dissatisfaction with the parties, the public and some
leaders have initiated several reforms or changes through the years.
One of the first reforms directed toward parties involved patronage
powers. Until the late 1800s the winning party was allowed to fill

governmental positions from top to bottom with party supporters and activists. The promise of public employment through party patronage served as a strong inducement to party fidelity and support. But the civil service reform movement swept through America, and government employment was reorganized under state and federal merit systems. Thus the parties were deprived of one of their strongest incentives for party support.

Unionization of government workers has also circumscribed the number of government jobs which can be manipulated by party officials who seek to reward the party faithful with public employment.

Nonpartisan Elections

Another defeat was dealt to parties by the reforms of a progressive movement active in the early 1900s which sought to eliminate partisanship in elections, especially at the local level. Proponents of nonpartisan elections equated party politics with corruption and political bossism. The effect of this movement was the atrophy of partisan elections at the local level of government. It has been argued that this weakened the two parties because it cut them off from their roots.

Direct Primaries

More recently the parties have been weakened in their role as electoral mechanisms. The advent of the direct primary was an initial step in this process. Direct primaries allow party followers to select party nominees in popular elections.

There are several types of direct primaries, some of which allow greater public participation than others. The effect of all such primaries, however, is to weaken the influence of party professionals over the nominating process. And when the role of party professionals and regulars is diminished, party organization ultimately suffers. With direct primaries, party elites can no longer meet in secret caucuses or small conventions to handpick the party's nominees for office. Without this nominating function, participation in party organization loses some of its attractiveness.

Candidate–Centered Campaigns

Party organizations have also lost some of their attraction for political candidates. Candidates quite naturally still pay some allegiance to party organization until they capture the party's nomination. But with a nomination in their grasp, candidates are increasingly deserting the party organization for campaign purposes and replacing it with a personal campaign organization.

The reasoning behind such strategy is not entirely clear. The consensus is, however, that an increasingly large bloc of independent voters prompts candidates to eschew party labels and personalize their campaigns. Also some critics have suggested that parties are not sophisticated enough in modern campaign techniques to appeal to the contemporary candidate. As Gelb and Palley have noted, "the role for parties diminishes as experts and technocrats gain public importance as purveyors of essential knowledge and skills."[32]

New Campaign Technology

The changing nature of campaigning and campaign technology has several facets. Robert Agranoff, a noted expert in the field of campaigning, points out that change has particularly altered the nature of campaign communications. He states that today the candidate, not the party, is the chief focus of campaign communications.[33] Many candidates completely eliminate any mention of their party affiliation in media messages. Agranoff notes further that party professionals no longer perform services for candidates in the area of communications. Instead, the candidate relies on the services of communications professionals who acquire their skills in nonpolitical fields.

Professional polling is another facet of the new campaign technology that has weakened the campaign role of parties. Polling results can determine the viability of a candidate's quest for a party's nomination. In the past, party professionals handpicked the "most promising" candidates and helped them secure the financial backing needed to seek a nomination. But today political financiers, the media, and even the public depend on poll results to narrow the field of potential party nominees.

The number of changes in campaign technology are endless, and only a few have been mentioned here. But the important lesson to be learned from these changes involves their impact on party organizations. Frank Sorauf has summarized this impact succinctly:

> All the campaign assets they (candidates) once received from the party organization and their workers—skills, information, pulse reading, manpower, exposure—they now can get from pollsters, the media, public relations people, volunteer workers, or even by "renting a party" in the form of a campaign management firm.[34]

The extent of increases in nonparty campaign management has been documented in several surveys. One such survey, conducted in 1972 and 1973, found that of 208 candidates running in statewide elections, 168 were employing at least one professional consultant in their campaign staffs. The same survey showed that 61 of 67 candidates for the U.S. Senate were using consultants.[35]

Convention Reform

Party organizations have also been weakened by national convention reforms, according to some observers. They suggest that recent reforms aimed at increasing participation by women and minorities at conventions have alienated many party regulars and professionals. Such charges seem to be exaggerated, though, at least in the Democratic Party.

Democratic Party convention reform efforts began in earnest following the uproarious Chicago convention of 1968. That occasion was best described by George McGovern:

> The Democratic National Convention of 1968 already has settled into the folklore of American politics. Its mere mention evokes the vision of tumultuous floor debate, bloodshed and tear gas in the streets, demonstrators and delegates standing together, arm–in–arm, in confrontation with the police. To some it also evokes the image of rigged procedures, of a political past assembled to reach predetermined decisions. The convention became the shame of the Democratic Party and in all likelihood assured its defeat in the November follow up. Wherever politicians meet—wherever Americans meet— they agree that the convention imposed such a strain on the democratic system of government that a repetition would be intolerable.[36]

Following the 1968 convention the McGovern Commission of the party recommended certain reforms that amounted to the use of quotas in selection of convention delegates. Women, blacks, and young people were given guarantees of more equitable representation. The result was a tumultuous convention again in 1972 which saw party regulars like Mayor Richard Daley of Chicago being forced from the convention floor in order to meet reform guidelines.

Some observers predicted that the ousted regulars would bolt the party or perhaps even try to destroy it. It was also thought by some that women and minorities who were gaining power would not be as committed to party organization. The argument was that the newcomers would place emphasis on further reform and strong issue stances instead of advocating party vitality.

Recent research reported by Dennis Sullivan, Jeffrey Pressman, and F. Christopher Arterton largely disproves such fears, however. Studying the 1974 Democratic Party Charter Conference, a sort of miniconvention, they found that representation by party professionals was greater than in 1972, which indicated that reform had not driven the regulars out of party decision making.[37]

A second observation by Sullivan's research team was that party reformers attending the 1974 conference were generally more committed to strengthening the national party organization than were the disgruntled regulars. One delegate, political scientist James MacGregor Burns, summed up the reformers' case:

> So the real issue at the miniconvention will not be between regulars and reformers, nor between liberals and conservatives nor between blacks and whites. It will be between those who believe in party organization in the best old–fashioned sense and those who don't care if the parties die because they will be happy in a nonparty politics of powerful personal campaign organizations.[38]

If this theme continues to permeate party reform, it will be erroneous to attribute party failures to the reform movement. It is also important to note that many of the reforms have been reversed. The Democrats, for example, now reserve convention seats for party office holders and other dignitaries. No longer will Democrats exclude officials like Chicago's late Mayor Daley under the new rules.

ALIENATION FROM PARTY

Recent studies by Jack Dennis make it clear that many Americans are alienated from the parties and the party system. Longitudinal analysis by Dennis suggests that trust in parties has gradually eroded since the time period analyzed in *The American Voter*.[39]

Alienation from parties takes several forms. Perhaps one of the most important representations of alienation involves a decline in citizens' willingness to place party above candidate. Dennis reports Gallup Poll data which show that in 1956, 22 percent of Americans believed "It is better to vote for the party than the man." By 1968, only 12 percent of a Gallup sample would express this same sentiment.

Dennis uses national SRC/CPS data and data collected in Wisconsin to demonstrate other trends:

1. There has been a sharp decline in public support for keeping party labels on election ballots (Wisconsin data, 1964–1974).
2. There has been a decline in public belief that parties help the government pay attention to what the people want (SRC/CPS data, 1964–1972).
3. There has been a decline in the numbers of citizens who feel that the parties are interested in more than people's votes (SRC/CPS data, 1968–1972).
4. Fewer persons believe that the political parties have done much good for "people like themselves" (Wisconsin data, 1972–1974).
5. Citizens believe that they have less say in what the political parties do (Wisconsin data, 1972–1974).
6. More citizens believe that the parties are in need of major change (Wisconsin data, 1972–1974).

The demise of public faith and confidence in political parties is best captured in data collected separately by Dennis and by Louis Harris which show that parties are held in much less regard than other political institutions. For example, Dennis asked nearly one thousand Wisconsin citizens: "How much faith and confidence would you say you had in each of these to do what is right?"[40] The respondents were asked to rank each of seven institutions between 1 (no confidence at all) and 7 (complete confidence). The mean scores for each institution are displayed in Table 2–6, along with the range of scores for political parties.

The mean confidence score for political parties, 3.8, is lower than for any other institution except interest groups.

Table 2–6
Confidence in Political Parties Relative to Other Institutions, 1974

How much faith and confidence would you say you had in each of these to do what is right? Using this scale, where 1 means no confidence at all and 7 means complete confidence, how much confidence do you have in . . . the political parties?

		1974
No confidence at all	1	7%
	2	9
	3	19
	4	34
	5	16
	6	8
Complete confidence	7	3
Not ascertained		4
Total		100%
N = 916		

1974 Mean Ratings

	X
Congress	4.6
Supreme Court	4.8
Presidency	4.3
Political parties	3.8
Elections	4.3
Interest groups	3.7
Federal administrative agencies	4.1

Source: Jack Dennis, "Trends in Support for the American Political Party System," paper presented at Annual Meeting of the American Political Science Association, Chicago, August–September, 1974.

Louis Harris found (in a 1973 national survey for the Senate Sub-committee on Intergovernmental Relations) that Americans are not likely to see parties as active or as agents of change.[41] For example, he asked respondents to name "groups of citizens and organizations which are most active" in their recent experience. Only 3 percent spontaneously mentioned political parties; by way of contrast, Ralph Nader's consumer group was mentioned by 7 percent. Local community groups, business groups, and church groups were all mentioned twice as often as political parties. Harris also asked respondents about actions they might take to change things they did not like about government. While two thirds agreed that working through a party was a possibility, more respondents indicated they would work through other groups or contact a relevant public official such as a senator or congressman.

Dennis also found in his Wisconsin surveys that respondents felt parties are in greater need of change than the Congress, the Supreme Court, the presidency, or even the federal bureaucracy.[42]

These findings present a rather bleak picture of public evaluation of parties. Dennis is correct when he notes that the base of support for parties is weak and "worsening with each passing year." And, he concludes:

> A mighty effort will therefore be required to reestablish the parties to the modicum of confidence and commitment that they enjoyed even a decade ago. Without such an effort, we may be called upon in the not so distant future to witness the demise of a once prominent institution of American government and politics.[43]

REALIGNMENT: THE NECESSARY CORRECTIVE?

Political scientists have long been interested in a phenomenon called *realignment*. Realignment occurs when there is a massive shift in the underlying pattern of partisan identification in the electorate. This change can be so sweeping that the majority party is transformed into a minority party and the minority party becomes the new majority party. The most recent example of a realignment took place during the 1930s, when the Democrats put together a large enough coalition (called the New Deal coalition) to overtake the Republicans in numerical strength and become the majority party.

Researchers have suggested two stimuli for realignment. Charles Sellars and others contend that realignments are cyclical phenomena.[44] Realignments lose their relevance after a more or less predictable period of time, coalitions disintegrate, and cyclical forces take charge to produce a new realignment. This ebb and flow was characterized by Sellars as an *equilibrium cycle* in two–party politics. A related stimulus for realignment is the appearance of some new issue or the advent of a national crisis, like war or depression, which causes a sudden transformation of partisan loyalties. V. O. Key characterized elections involving such occurrences as *critical elections.*[45]

In recent years researchers have been looking for the signs of impending realignment. Numerous scholars have indicated that the following occurrences are indicative of the collapse of the New Deal coalition and a coming realignment: (1) the increase in independents, (2) the success of third parties, (3) the increase in issue voting, and (4) declining confidence in the parties as they are presently constituted.

Paul Beck has suggested further that parents of new voters are not transmitting family partisanship to their children today with the same "efficiency" that characterized partisan transmission immediately following the New Deal. Richard Trilling finds that voters, especially among the young, are less prone to use New Deal symbols in making candidate and party evaluations. Norman Nie, Sidney Verba, and John Petrocik, as well as Everett Ladd and Charles Hadley, have concluded that the social group foundations of the New Deal coalition are crumbling.[46]

The conclusion drawn from these trends is summarized well by Jerome Clubb, William Flanigan, and Nancy Zingale: "Taken together, this evidence suggests a considerable growth in the size of the pool of voters without well–developed partisan loyalties. Most analysts . . . see this as indicative of an increasing availability of potential new partisans in a realignment."[47] These authors express doubt, however, that a realignment will actually occur because a necessary component of the realigning process is missing. They contend that realignment can occur only after a party perceived as unsuccessful in governing is replaced by a party which is ultimately perceived as successful in governing where the former party failed. Because "successful" governance today would require control of all branches of the government simultaneously (something only the Democrats might accomplish in the near term), and because government's problems might be unsolvable, at least to the public's satisfaction, the requirement for realignment is not likely to be met.

The greatest amount of research directed toward predicting and explaining realignment has dealt with the South. The South has been interesting in this regard because the supposed "solid Democratic South" generally supported the Republican presidential nominees in 1964, 1968, and 1972. This prompted some Republicans to anticipate achieving a "New Majority" status for their party as the South gradually turned away from the Democrats and joined their more conservative allies in the GOP.

There have been several explanations of partisan change in the South. James Sundquist has suggested that a *new* realignment is not occurring in the South. Rather, he sees the the South belatedly conforming to class–based patterns of partisanship adopted by the rest of the nation in the New Deal realignment of the 1930s. This explanation envisions middle– and upper–class white Southerners becoming Republican in partisan orientation.[48] Research conducted by Carol Cassel tends to refute Sundquist's thesis. In her study of native white Southerners over the period 1952–1972, she found that group moving away from its traditional Democratic partisanship toward the independent, not Republican, label.[49]

Another perspective on change in the South has been adopted by Philip Converse. He attributes most change in Southern partisanship not to political conversions, but instead to the relocation of northern Republicans as industry and commerce move south of the Mason–Dixon Line.[50]

Of course, all of these interpretations must await further evaluation following Jimmy Carter's sweeping Democratic victory in the South in 1976. While Reagan did bring most of the South back into the GOP column in 1980, Carter's initial ability to woo voters as a Democrat may indicate that many Southerners are ready to return to their historical partisan allegiance if the Democrats provide them with a suitable candidate as they did in nominating Carter in 1976, a fellow southerner. Whether nonsouthern Democrats can win southern Democrats' votes again remains to be seen.

So while the prospects for realignment seem tentative, the prospects for other outcomes are enhanced. An often–discussed possible outcome is continued *dealignment,* culminating in the possible collapse of the parties as we know them. Dealignment involves the electorate's psychological and behavioral rejection of parties, a move we have noted throughout this chapter. Predictions of doom for parties are shared by many prominent political scientists, including Burnham, and Nie, Verba, and Petrocik. The latter coauthors have concluded that there is "little prospect for the emergence of a new party system from the disarray for the present system."[51] But all political scientists do not agree with this conclusion, and we are included in this group.

A TREND ASSESSMENT: PARTISANSHIP

At the conclusion of this and the next two chapters we will offer assessments of selected aspects of each trend under consideration. These assessments focus on some of the more controversial aspects of contemporary political science. The original research discussed here should help students and other researchers better understand the various phenomena of change in the American electorate.

We will seek to assess changes in the American electorate over time on five variables: (1) voting defection from party identification, (2) the nature of independency, (3) quality of candidate evaluation, (4) participation, and (5) alienation or loss of trust. The first three are introduced in this chapter.

We use party identification to measure the first two of our five trend variables: defection from party identification and nature of independency. In voting for president, defection or loyalty depends on the correspondence between one's party identification and the party of the candidate for which one votes. For example, a Democrat who voted for Ronald Reagan in 1980 would be defecting from the party, as Reagan was the Republican candidate. A vote for Jimmy Carter would have been a loyal vote.

The question arises as to how to treat independents who admit to leaning toward the Democrats or the Republicans. Since SRC/CPS research has shown that such "partisan" independents vote overwhelmingly for the candidates of the party toward which they lean, we included them as possible defectors.

In 1980 both those who considered themselves Republicans or Democrats could defect from their party in one of two ways: they could vote for the candidate of the other major party or they could vote for John Anderson who ran as an independent (or for one of the other minor candidates). Not surprisingly, few strong partisans did either. But as we can see in Table 2–7, many weak partisans and leaners were tempted to defect and vote for a candidate not nominated by their party. (It is apparent that the Democrats experienced this much more than did the Republicans). A comparison of weak partisans and leaners shows clearly that supposedly independent leaners were no more likely to defect to the other major political party candidate than were weak partisans, although leaners were drawn in larger numbers to Anderson. Since it is only the occasional presidential election that offers a serious third choice of candidates, it appears that for most elections there is little that is truly "independent" about the leaners. Most vote very much like partisans, at least like the weak ones.

Table 2-7
Presidential Vote by Party
Identification, 1980

| | Percent voted for: | | | |
	Reagan	Carter	Anderson	Others
Strong Democrat	11	86	3	—
Weak Democrat	33	60	8	—
Leaning Democrat	29	45	20	6
Independent	64	22	12	2
Leaning Republican	76	12	10	3
Weak Republican	86	5	9	1
Strong Republican	92	5	4	—

Note: N = 968
Source: SRC/CPS Election Study

As we saw in Table 2-1, both major political parties have lost weak and strong supporters to the ranks of independents. But more than one-half of the increasingly numerous independents admit to leaning toward one of the two parties. And most of these leaners continue to vote for the nominee of the party toward which they lean. Therefore, we have elected to refer only to *pure* independents in our evaluation of the increase in independency. Only these pure independents reflect a significant change from the politics of the 1950s. Considering only pure independents make the magnitude of the trend toward increasing independence less dramatic, but pure independents alone seem to merit consideration as voters free from party ties.

Quality of Candidate Evaluation

The third variable to be introduced in this chapter is quality of candidate evaluation. Many central questions concerning the American electorate involve the quality of the decision underlying the voter's choice of presidential candidates. Much of the controversy concerning the implications of studies of the electorate center on whether issues or candidates' images are now the most important determinant of how people vote. Have positions on issues as taken by candidates and as preferred by voters replaced party loyalty in voting? Or is the image of the candidates, especially trivial aspects such as sense of humor or physical attractiveness, as manipulated in media presentations, now central to the voter's decision among candidates?

Our measure of the quality of a voter's evaluation of a presidential candidate uses questions asked in the SRC/CPS studies since 1952. In each instance, respondents were queried as to whether there was anything which would cause them to vote for or against the Democratic or Republican candidates for president. We scanned three possible responses for pro–Democratic, con–Democratic, pro–Republican, and con–Republican reactions to the candidates to ascertain a hierarchy or rank ordering of quality in these responses.

If any one of the possible twelve responses revealed a mention of an ideological standard for candidate evaluation, such as "He is too liberal," that respondent is credited with giving the most sophisticated response and labeled *ideologue*. The next lower level of candidate evaluation involves mention of an issue, such as "He favors Medicare." Respondents who evaluate candidates in these terms are assigned the label *issue-oriented*. If a respondent gives neither of these types of responses, but instead sees a candidate in terms of the groups the candidate will place at an advantage or disadvantage, such as "He will hurt the farmers," the respondent is labeled *group benefits* in orientation. Next lower in quality of evaluation is the respondent who sees the candidates in terms of the political party they represent, such as, "He is a good Democrat." Such a respondent is labeled *partisan*.

The last two classes of candidate evaluation lack any evidence that the voter prefers a candidate because of a policy preference espoused by the candidate. The voter who mentions some assessment of a candidate's personality, such as "He looks honest," or "I like him," is labeled an *image* evaluator. The class labeled *no content* is the lowest rung on our hierarchy of quality of evaluation. Such respondents give *no* response to any question concerning the candidates for president. Obviously, evaluations by ideologues and issue–oriented voters reflect a quality which suggests their choice among the candidates could lead to the enactment of policies they prefer. They are judged high quality on this basis. The image and no–content evaluators are judged low quality, as no issue positions are furthered by a candidate receiving their vote.

Our use of these categories of candidate evaluation suggests that were the electorate as a whole to exhibit substantially more concern about issues, survey responses as to why voters have decided to vote for or against candidates should reveal this improvement. Certainly, one could argue for new questions which might better measure the issue sophistication of the average voter, and certainly other existing questions can be used to make an assessment. But because these questions are open ended, taking the respondent's own words as an answer, they neither suggest answers nor force the respondent to choose between a limited number of possible answers. Furthermore, by structuring a hierarchy of responses in which the respondent is credited for his or her *most sophisticated response,* we allow every opportunity for a more ideologically sophisticated, issue–voting electorate to reveal itself.[52]

Table 2–8 shows that in 1980, some 58 percent of the electorate revealed highest quality candidate evaluations (10 percent ideologue and 48 percent issue–oriented), while 34 percent gave the lowest quality evaluations (22 percent image and 12 percent no content). Scanning the trend in highest quality evaluation since 1952 indicates fluctuations from the low of 17 percent in 1952 to a high of 58 percent in 1980. Substantial declines in 1968 and 1976, however, suggest the absence of a continuous trend. Were 1964, 1972, and 1980 merely peaks, to be followed by a return to 1950 levels? All that can be said with complete confidence is that the pattern of issue–oriented responses is very erratic.

But low–quality evaluations show a consistent decline, from a high in 1952 of 77 percent (62 percent image and 15 percent no content) to 34 percent in 1980. The consistency of this decline is entirely a function of the consistent decline of image–only responses by respondents. No–content responses show no pattern of change.

Partisan responses were common only in 1968 and 1976 and thus seemingly unrelated to other types of evaluations.

High Quality Independents?   Figure 2–4 clearly reveals that the pattern noted in Table 2–8 holds regardless of whether the respondent is a Democrat, a Republican, or an independent. If any such pattern of difference between independents and partisans is notable, it is that between 1960 and 1980 independents showed very slightly lower quality evaluations than did partisans. In 1956 they were slightly higher. The improvement in quality of candidate evaluation is not unique to independents. Indeed, it has affected them somewhat less!

Table 2-8
Trend in Quality of Candidate Evaluations, 1952–1980

			Percentage of Respondents Using Various Types of Candidate Evaluations				
	Ideologue	Issue Oriented	Group Benefit	Partisan	Image	No Content	N
1952	1%	16%	5%	1%	62%	15%	1,899
1956	1	19	6	—	64	10	1,762
1960	1	20	4	—	62	12	1,181
1964	6	35	5	—	44	9	1,571
1968	3	23	5	19	36	15	1,557
1972	7	44	5	6	28	10	1,372
1976	7	35	9	13	27	9	2,870
1980	10	48	3	5	22	12	1,614

Source: SRC/CPS Election Studies.

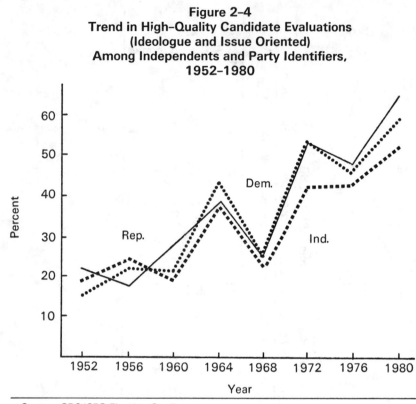

Figure 2–4
Trend in High–Quality Candidate Evaluations
(Ideologue and Issue Oriented)
Among Independents and Party Identifiers,
1952–1980

Source: SRC/CPS Election Studies.

Are Defectors Higher Quality Evaluators?   Defection among partisans in voting for president has varied substantially across elections. In 1952, 22 percent of all partisans (those identifying with a political party or leaning toward it) defected to the opposition party in voting for president. Defection then declined to a low of 14 percent in 1960, followed by a rise to yet another peak in 1972 at 27 percent. Clubb, Flanigan, and Zingale have shown that this rise is almost exclusively due to southern Democrats who cast their votes for Goldwater, Wallace, and Nixon between 1964 and 1972. In 1976 defection sharply declined to 17 percent only to peak once again in 1980 when about one–third of all partisans defected.[53] The percentages of defection are:

1952	....	22%
1956	....	17%
1960	....	14%
1964	....	16%
1968	....	25%
1972	....	27%
1976	....	17%
1980	....	33%

No trend line is apparent in these data, meaning that the best prediction of what the rate of defection will be in the 1980s is between 14 and 33 percent, or the mean of 21 percent. Whatever other factors influence the American electorate, eight out of ten partisans continue to vote loyally for their party's nominee for president. The high rates of defection observed in 1968 and 1980 suggest that this is most true when a popular third–party candidate seeks the presidency.

Defectors show no unique increase in the quality of their candidate evaluations. Figure 2–5 distinguishes between those who defect in their presidential vote and those who defect locally for senator or representative. Four types of voters are thus shown: (1) those defecting in the presidential election and for at least one of the local offices (*DD* on the figure), (2) presidential defectors and local loyalists (*DL*), (3) presidential loyalists and local defectors (*LD*), and (4) total loyalists (*LL*). Local defectors during the period 1952–1964 proved somewhat higher in quality in the candidate evaluations. But all voters seem nearly identically affected by the somewhat jagged trend toward higher quality in candidate evaluations.

Conclusion

In this chapter we have considered two different aspects of the American electorate's involvement with political parties, willingness to identify with one of the parties, and, given that willingness, loyalty to the party in voting for its nominees. If unwillingness to identify with a political party were more common, with an increasing number of citizens declaring themselves independent of parties, and if defection in voting were growing among the remaining partisans, we might well explain such trends by questioning the usefulness of parties in influenc-

ing how people vote. The possibility that voters have perceived the
parties as failing to reflect issue divisions felt by an increasingly issue–
oriented public would seem to be a viable explanation. But our assessment of trends over this 28–year period refutes this explanation in two
ways.

Figure 2-5
Trend in High Quality Candidate Evaluation
(Ideologue and Issue Oriented),
Among Defectors and Loyalists,
1952–1980

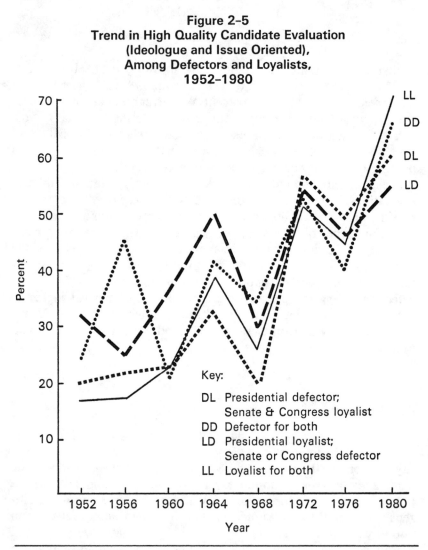

Key:

DL Presidential defector;
    Senate & Congress loyalist
DD Defector for both
LD Presidential loyalist;
    Senate or Congress defector
LL Loyalist for both

Source: SRC/CPS Election Studies.

First, while independents are more numerous (12 percent in 1980 versus 5 percent in 1952; see Table 2–1), defections show no consistent pattern of increase. (Presidential voting defection in 1976 was the same, 17 percent, among partisans that it was in 1956.) Perhaps even more conclusively, these data show that neither refusing to identify with a political party nor defection in voting from one's political party relates to the sophistication one shows in evaluation of presidential candidates. Voter sophistication, as judged by the use of issues or ideology in evaluating the candidates, has improved, but it is neither the cause nor the result of disenchantment of the public with the major political parties.

The majority political party in terms of identifications, the Democrats, may have lost five of the eight presidential elections during this period, but no growth in the number of Republicans is evident in the electorate. It remains the case that about 88 percent of the electorate are partisans, and about eight out of ten partisans vote for their party's presidential candidate. Since a relatively constant 60 percent of partisans are Democrats, a typical Democratic presidential candidate can expect to receive slightly over 40 percent of the vote out of partisan loyalty. A Republican candidate, by contrast, can expect only about 28 percent of the vote out of the same apparent motivation. Obviously, both need to pursue possible defectors and independents to win, but the Republican must try harder. Deviations from this overall pattern are not likely to occur in the near future, if the past is any guide. Only substantial changes in the nature of partisanship and independency, or the nature of candidate evaluations, is likely to alter election outcomes.

POSTSCRIPT: THE FUTURE OF PARTIES IN AMERICA

E. E. Schattschneider once advanced the thesis that "the political parties created democracy and that modern democracy is unthinkable save in terms of parties."[54] Such an expression represents the thoughts and concerns of political scientists who are troubled about the future of parties.

Our own assessment of the future of parties in America coincides with that of Jack Dennis when he argues that "some clouds are beginning to form; but the storm has not fully arrived."[55] The parties may yet avoid what many researchers see as an inevitable collision with infamy and disestablishment.

Our guarded optimism for the future of American political parties is based in part upon a feeling that some researchers have exaggerated the roles that increasing independency and issue voting may play in weakening the parties. As Jerome Clubb and his associates have stated: "It is one thing to observe that these tendencies exist at the present time and a considerably stronger contention that these tendencies reveal the demise of political parties."[56]

The logic behind Clubb's statement is demonstrated by critical evaluation of the trend in independent identification. It is indeed true that more and more Americans eschew the traditional party labels in favor of an independent label. But many such persons remain "closet partisans," leaning toward a party if not initially admitting to identifying with one. Such closet partisanship still influences candidate choices. So partisanship continues to play a role, even for the increasing numbers of independents.

Parties are also showing some aptitude for responding to their organizational crises as well. The Democrats, for example, registered about 3.1 million new voters before the 1976 election. About 80 percent of these registered as Democratic partisans. Such registration drives demonstrated that the parties still have the capacity for growth. The Republicans have developed an in–house political consulting capacity which rivals some of the better private media and organizational consultants.

Parties also were benefited by the Campaign Finance Act of 1974, which provided for public financing of the presidential campaigns of the two major parties' nominees. Third–party efforts are discouraged. Also, because political donors, "fat cats," could not heavily contribute to the presidential campaigns under this 1974 law, many gave donations instead to the national party organizations. Such financial good fortune has helped the parties regain fiscal integrity and provides the basis for renewed party programs at the state and national levels.

So the parties will survive. And partisanship will continue to be a dynamic force in American politics. Perhaps the role of parties will not be as important as it was found to be by the authors of *The American Voter* and other early electoral studies. But it is still much too early to proclaim that "the party is over."

NOTES

1. David Broder, *The Party's Over* (New York: Harper & Row, 1972).
2. Perhaps the best summary of the literature on party decline is William J. Crotty and Gary C. Jacobson, *American Parties in Decline* (Boston: Little, Brown, 1980); also see Gerald M. Pomper, *Voters' Choice* (New York: Dodd, Mead & Co., 1975); Walter Dean Burnham, *Critical Elections and the Mainsprings of American Politics* (New York: W. W. Norton, 1970); Walter DeVries and V. Lance Tarrance, *The Ticket Splitter: A New Force in American Politics* (Grand Rapids, Mich.: William B. Eerdmans Publishing Co., 1972); Jack Dennis, "Trends in Support for the American Political Party System" (Paper presented at Annual Meeting of the American Political Science Association, Chicago, August–September 1974).
3. Dennis, "Trends in Support for Party Systems;" *Gallup Opinion Index* and *Gallup Opinion Report,* various issues; Stephen D. Shaffer, "A Multivariate Explanation of Rising Ticketsplitting" (Paper presented at the annual meeting of the Southern Political Science Association, Atlanta, 1982).
4. DeVries and Tarrance, *Ticket Splitter,* pp. 30–33.
5. Ruth K. Scott and Ronald J. Hrebenar, *Parties in Crisis* (New York: John Wiley and Sons, 1979), pp. 145–46.
6. V. O. Key, Jr., *The Responsible Electorate* (Cambridge, Mass.: Belknap Pres., 1966).
7. Ibid., Chap. 2.
8. Philip E. Converse et al., "Stability and Change in 1960: A Reinstating Election," in *Elections and the Political Order,* eds. Angus Campbell, Philip E. Converse, Warren E. Miller, and Donald E. Stokes (New York: John Wiley & Sons, 1966), p. 83.
9. Key, *Responsible Electorate,* p. 64.
10. Ibid., p. 65.
11. Ibid., p. 71.
12. Pomper, *Voters' Choice,* p. 33.
13. Correlation coefficients, such as those used by Burnham here, are statistics which help explain the strength of a relationship between two phenomena. In this case Burnham is matching partisan percentages of the presidential vote for each state with similar percentages for each state in the following presidential election. Thus the coefficients tell us something about the magnitude of party support from one election to the next. The correlations could range from 0.00 to 1.00, with the "normal" range for these coefficients falling somewhere between 0.90 and 1.00, according to Burnham. Lower correlation coefficients would indicate large differences in party support in many of the states from one presidential election the next.
14. Burnham, *Critical Elections and Mainsprings of Politics,* p. 167.
15. Angus Campbell, Philip E. Converse, Warren E. Miller, and Donald E.

Stokes, *The American Voter* (Chicago: University of Chicago Press, 1960):
Chap. 8, pp. 168–87.

16.   Ibid., p. 249.

17.   Stanley Freedman, "American Presidential Elections: Issues and Voter
Motivation" Ph.D. diss., The Florida State University, 1975), p. 24.

18.   Martin Luther King, Jr., "Letter from Birmingham City Jail," in *The
Few and The Many*, eds. Thomas R. Dye and Harmon Zeigler (Belmont, Calif.:
Duxbury Press, 1972), pp. 213–20.

19.   Philip E. Converse, "Change in the American Electorate," in *The Human
Meaning of Social Change*, eds. Angus Campbell and Philip E. Converse (New
York: Russell Sage Foundation, 1972), pp. 322–23.

20.   Pomper, *Voters' Choice*, chap. 8.

21.   Ibid., p. 168.

22.   William Schneider, "1980—A Watershed Year," *Politics Today* 7, no.
1 (January/February, 1980): 30.

23.   Pomper, *Voter's Choice*, p. 173.

24.   Philip E. Converse, "The Nature of Belief Systems in Mass Publics,"
in *Ideology and Discontent*, ed. David Apter (Glencoe, Ill.: Free Press, 1964).

25.   Norman H. Nie with Kristi Anderson, "Mass Belief Systems Revisited:
Political Change and Attitude Structure," *Journal of Politics*, 36 (August 1974):
540–91.

26.   Arthur H. Miller, Warren W. Miller, Alden S. Raine, and Thad A.
Brown, "A Majority Party in Disarray: Policy Polarization in the 1972 Election," *American Political Science Review* 70 (September 1976): 753–78.

27.   Nie with Anderson, "Mass Belief Systems Revisited."

28.   John L. Sullivan, James E. Pierson, and George E. Marcus, "Ideological
Constraint in the Mass Public: A Methodological Critique and Some New
Findings," *American Journal of Political Science* 22 (May 1978): 233–49; George
F. Bishop, Alfred J. Tuchfarber, and Robert W. Oldendick, "Change in the
Structure of American Political Attitudes: The Nagging Question of Question
Wording," *American Journal of Political Science* 22 (May 1978): 250–69; Philip
E. Converse and Gregory B. Markus, "Plus Ça Change: The New CPS Election
Study Panel," *American Political Science Review*, 73 (March 1979): 32–49.

29.   Robert S. Erikson, Norman R. Luttbeg, and Kent L. Tedin, *American
Public Opinion*, 2d ed. (New York: John Wiley & Sons, 1980), Chap. 3.

30.   Eugene DeClercq, Thomas L. Hurley, and Norman R. Luttbeg, "Voting
in American Presidential Elections: 1956–1972," in *American Electoral Behavior: Change and Stability*, ed. Samuel A. Kirkpatrick (Beverly Hills, Calif.: Sage
Publications, 1976), pp. 9–33.

31.   Joyce Gelb and Marian Lief Palley, *Tradition and Change in American
Party Politics* (New York: Thomas Y. Crowell Co., 1975), p. 3.

32.   Ibid., p. 4.

33.   Robert Agranoff, *The Management of Election Campaigns* (Boston:
Holbrook Press, 1976), p. 17.

34. Frank J. Sorauf, *Party Politics in America*, 3rd ed. (Boston: Little, Brown & Co., 1976), pp. 416–17.

35. *The New York Times*, November 5, 1970, p. 28.

36. George McGovern, "The Lessons of 1968," *Harper's Magazine*, January 1970, p. 43.

37. Dennis G. Sullivan, Jeffrey L. Pressman, and F. Christopher Arterton, *Explorations in Convention Decision Making: The Democratic Party in the 1970s* (San Francisco: W. H. Freeman, 1976).

38. Ibid., p. 43. Originally appeared in "Kansas City Scenario," by James MacGregor Burns, *The Washington Post*, December 5, 1974.

39. Dennis, "Trends in Support for Party System."

40. Ibid., pp. 23–24.

41. U.S. Congress, Senate, Committee on Government Operations, *Confidence and Concern: Citizens View American Government*, 93rd Cong., 1st Sess., December 3, 1973.

42. Dennis, "Trends in Support for Party System," pp. 14–15.

43. Ibid., p. 24.

44. Charles Sellars, "The Equilibrium Cycle in Two Party Politics," *Public Opinion Quarterly* 29 (Spring 1965): 16–38.

45. V. O. Key, Jr., "A Theory of Critical Elections," *Journal of Politics* 17 (February 1955): 3–18. Also see Gerald Pomper, "A Classification of Presidential Elections," *Journal of Politics* 29 (August 1967): 535–66.

46. Paul Beck, "A Socialization Theory of Partisan Realignment," in *The Politics of Future Citizens*, eds. Richard G. Niemi and Associates (San Francisco: Jossey–Bass Publishers, 1974), pp. 199–219; Paul Beck, "Youth and the Politics of Realignment," in *Political Opinion and Behavior*, eds. E. C. Dreyer and W. A. Rosenbaum (Belmont, Calif.: Wadsworth Publishing Co., 1976), pp. 366–73; Richard J. Trilling, "Party Image and Partisan Change, " in *The Future of Political Parties*, eds. Louis Maisel and Paul M. Sacks (Beverly Hills, Calif.: Sage Publications, 1975), pp. 63–100; Norman H. Nie, Sidney Verba, and John R. Petrocik, *The Changing American Voter* (Cambridge, Mass.: Harvard University Press, 1976), Chap. 14; Everett Carll Ladd, Jr., with Charles D. Hadley, *Transformations of the American Party System* (New York: W. W. Norton & Co., 1975); E. C. Ladd, Jr., *Where Have All the Voters Gone?* (New York: W. W. Norton & Co., 1978).

47. Jerome M. Clubb, William H. Flanigan, and Nancy H. Zingale, "Partisan Realignment Since 1960." (Paper presented at the 1976 meeting of the American Political Science Association, Chicago, p. 7.)

48. James Sundquist, *Dynamics of the Party System* (Washington, D.C.: Brookings Institution, 1973).

49. Carol Cassel, "Cohort Analysis of Party Identification among Southern Whites, 1952–1972," *Public Opinion Quarterly* 41 (1977): 28–33.

50. Philip E. Converse, "On the Possibility of a Major Realignment in the South," in *Elections and the Political Order*, eds. Angus Campbell, et al. (New York: John Wiley & Sons, 1966).

51.   Nie, Verba, and Petrocik, *Changing American Voter,* p. 354.

52.   This decision was made out of agreement with John Kessel's admonition that changes in issue voting in the American electorate can only be noted if the methodology for assessing such voting is held constant. Otherwise, it may well be the methodology which causes the changes: John H. Kessel, "Comment: The Issues in Issue Voting," *American Political Science Review,* June 1972, pp. 459–65. For various reasons scholars have focused on consistency in public attitudes on national issues as an indicator of the evaluative capabilities of the electorate. Unfortunately, there has not been a continuing and constant method of assessing these attitudes across the years. Thus, changes in consistency seem mainly the result of changing methodology rather than a changing electorate. Our earlier decision thus seems well justified. See: George F. Bishop et al., "Change in the Structure of American Political Attitudes: The Nagging Question of Question Wording," *American Journal of Political Science* 22 (May 1978): 250–69; and John L. Sullivan, James E. Pierson, and George E. Marcus, "Ideological Constraint in the Mass Public: A Methodological Critique and Some New Findings," *American Journal of Political Science* 22 (May 1978): 233–49.

53.   Clubb et al., "Partisan Realignment since 1960."

54.   E. E. Schattschneider, *Party Government* (New York: Rinehart, 1942), p. 1.

55.   Dennis, "Trends in Support for Party System," p. 5.

56.   Clubb et al., "Partisan Realignment since 1960," p. 13.

CHAPTER 3

The Decline In Political Participation

In this chapter we will analyze trends in political participation since *The American Voter,* as well as trends in voting turnout over a longer time span—beginning in the last century and continuing to the 1982 congressional election. Pre-1950s voting can be documented without opinion survey data using election statistics published by the Bureau of the Census and state governments, but these statistics do not provide adequate information as to *why* people vote. For recent elections, opinion survey data are available to assist in interpreting the attitudinal correlates of voting and nonvoting.

In the latter part of this chapter we will look at political participation other than voting. While voting in presidential elections is the only participatory act engaged in by a majority of Americans, it is important to consider other types of participation in order to understand fully trends in political activism.

DEFINING AND MEASURING ELECTORAL TURNOUT

Voting turnout is a concept with a multitude of meanings and measurements. The first consideration to be made in defining turnout involves identifying the potential electorate. The electorate could be defined as all persons officially registered to vote. However, in most instances in this book and others, the *potential electorate* includes all persons who are of voting age (now, at least 18) regardless of their registration status. Voting turnout is therefore usually defined as the proportion of persons of legal voting age who actually vote in a given election.

A second consideration in defining turnout is how it is actually measured. One way is simply to use official turnout counts reported by the government and media. This approach has one major drawback, however. If we want to study *attitudes* related to voting and nonvoting, we cannot relate the concepts using official vote tabulations. Instead, we must ask a sampling of persons whether they voted and then proceed to pose additional attitude questions to the same sample of people.

Thus far we have identified two methods for measuring turnout, or the proportion of eligible persons actually voting. The first method uses official counts. We will call this the *actual turnout*. A second method of measurement involves estimating turnout from a sample survey. This method results in what we will call *reported turnout.*

While reported turnout is invaluable to political scientists, it poses some very real problems as well. The primary problem is that reported turnout figures almost always exceed by a wide margin actual turnout figures for the same election. For example, actual turnout estimates for the 1976 presidential election show that about 54 percent of the electorate voted. But a sample survey of the electorate conducted after the 1976 election indicated that 59 percent of the electorate had voted. Thus the reported turnout exceeded the actual turnout by nearly 5 percent.

This problem is further illustrated in Figure 3–1, which gives actual turnout in the 1972 presidential election and several reported turnout figures taken from polls and opinion surveys conducted after the election. You can readily determine that reported turnout data are not terribly accurate. The census survey came closest to the actual figure, but it was still off by over 7 percent. The SRC/CPS and Louis Harris and Associates surveys were off by a whopping 17 percent.

Why is reported turnout so inaccurate? The problem certainly does not stem from any lack of expertise on the part of the researchers who publish the data. The SRC/CPS and Harris researchers are recognized as some of the best in survey research. A more likely fault with reported turnout stems from the tendency of many Americans to report having voted when, in actuality, they did not.

The rationale for persons overreporting their voting is complex. Some may not want to admit to interviewers that voting, an aspect of civic duty, was ignored or neglected. Another stimulus to overreporting

Figure 3-1
Actual and Reported Turnouts for 1972 Presidential Election

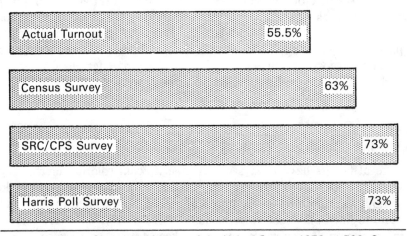

Source: Actual, *Statistical Abstract of the United States: 1978,* p. 520; Census Survey, U.S. Bureau of the Census, *Current Population Reports,* Series P–20, No. 332; SRC/CPS Survey, 1972 SRC/CPS Election Study; Harris Poll Survey, *Confidence and Concern: Citizens View American Government,* data collected September 1973.

occurs in Census Bureau surveys when one member of a household is asked to report on the voting behavior of an absent family member, like a child at college. Thus a father, giving his son the benefit of any doubt, may tell the interviewer that a son away from home at college did vote in the last election when, in fact, the son did not vote at all.

There are at least two other important reasons for the lack of correspondence between actual turnout and reported turnout. First, surveys do not include persons who are permanent transients or are institutionalized. Because these persons would not normally vote, their exclusion from surveys can cause an overestimate of up to 5 percent in reported turnout, according to Louis Harris and Associates. Finally, in every election a large number of persons do vote only to have their votes later invalidated and excluded from the official count. Invalidation of votes results from improper voting practices such as voting for more than one candidate for the same office. According to Hugh Bone and Austin Ranney, "The Survey Research Center estimates that about 2 percent of the votes cast in presidential elections are regularly invalidated by election officials . . . ; in (presidential election years) a loss of nearly 3 million votes."[1]

FACTORS WHICH INFLUENCE VOTER PARTICIPATION

The list of factors thought to have some impact on voter turnout is almost endless. Influences on turnout are generally organized under three major headings: (1) legal factors, (2) psychological factors, and (3) personal or demographic factors. We will elaborate on specific aspects of each category, and then analyze the comparative degree of influence each of these factors has exerted on turnout since 1952.

The Law And Voter Turnout

Legal factors have always played a significant role in determining who can or cannot vote, as well as who does vote once qualified. While some laws, especially at the state level, have been passed through the years to limit universal voter participation severely, the overall trend in legislation and court decisions has been to encourage voting. The changes since our nation's founding are astounding. It has been estimated that in 1789 "only about one of every thirty adult Americans (mostly propertied white males) was legally eligible to vote."[2] Today only a few adult Americans are legally barred from voting.

The remaining legal restrictions on universal suffrage are noncontroversial and unlikely to be changed. One exception is the requirement in many states that potential voters register in person thirty days or more before a given election. Former President Jimmy Carter and others have advocated a national policy which allows registration up to and including the day of an election. Legal barriers to voting which are likely to remain unchanged include prohibitions on voting by convicted felons, inmates of correctional institutions, and persons adjudged to be mentally incompetent. There have been some much-publicized attempts by prison inmates to run for public office, but these have been more publicity seeking than philosophical in nature.

Certain changes in electoral laws have affected turnout. Historical data show that voter turnout reached an apex in the presidential election of 1876. In that election over 85 percent of the eligible electorate voted. Throughout the middle to the late nineteenth century voter participation was high. But the election of 1896 marked a dramatic downturn in electoral participation.

Several legal developments are linked to this decline in turnout, from which the electorate has never fully recovered. Philip Converse, Jerrold Rusk, and to a lesser extent Walter Dean Burnham, have hypothesized that declining turnout was a result of the advent of voter registration laws enacted around the turn of the century.[3] Prior to such laws persons were allowed to vote, without registration, on their own pledge that they were residents of the community. Most persons were readily recognizable in small communities, but as society became more urban and mobile, the lack of registration led to widespread voting fraud. There was nothing to prevent a voter from casting ballots at several polling places. The unfortunate results of efforts to fight such fraud was a downturn of "significant numbers of legitimate voters" at the polls.[4]

Another legal development that may have caused a decline in turnout was ratification of the Nineteenth Amendment to the Constitution in 1920. This amendment gave the vote to women, thus potentially doubling the electorate. Once given the vote, however, women were slow to use their new privilege. This is typical of any newly enfranchised group. A period of socialization must normally transpire before any new group's turnout equals that of the rest of the electorate. The difference between male and female turnout has closed in recent years.

Poll Taxes and Literacy and Constitution Tests. Laws having an impact on the turnout of black Americans have both aided and thwarted their participation in American elections. Blacks were first given the vote nationally with the passage of the Fifteenth Amendment to the Constitution in 1870, but as Reconstruction governments were dismantled in the South, Southern legislators moved to pass laws which discouraged or prohibited black voting. The exit of blacks from the electorate contributed to the post–1900 decline in voting.

State legislatures in the South employed a wide variety of legal limitations on black registration and voting. These included poll taxes, literacy tests, tests on understanding of the Constitution, and rigorous residency and registration requirements. The dominant Democratic Party also excluded blacks from the political process through the use of its all–white primary elections. We will describe these restrictive practices and their legal or judicial remedies below.

Poll taxes were small fees, usually two or three dollars, charged to voters in an election. While this practice discriminated against the generally impoverished black population, it also prohibited many poor whites from voting. Because of this, many states voluntarily eliminated the poll tax in favor of other restrictions on black voting. But, because of the persistence of the poll tax in five states, the Twenty-fourth Amendment was adopted in 1964. The amendment only affected national government elections, so the Congress authorized, in the 1965 Voting Rights Act, a court test of poll taxes for state and local office elections. The Supreme Court declared *all* poll taxes unconstitutional in its subsequent 1966 judicial decision, *Harper v. Virginia State Board of Elections.*

Literacy tests and "understanding the Constitution" tests were also powerful tools used to disenfranchise blacks. These tests were very powerful, according to Jack Plano and Milton Greenberg, because:

> ... examining officials have great discretion, especially when the tests are administered orally. In some southern states, for example, Negro college graduates were once disqualified because they failed to interpret constitutional passages to the satisfaction of a white board of examiners.[5]

The Voting Rights Act of 1965 also imposed a five–year suspension on the use of literacy tests. When this act was renewed in 1970, literacy tests were, in effect, permanently suspended in local, state, or national elections. The Supreme Court upheld the suspension in a 1970 decision, *Oregon v. Mitchell.*

For a while blacks were excluded from the Southern electorate because of "whites only" Democratic party primary elections. Democratic primaries were tantamount to general elections in the South because Republicans almost never fielded candidates in the regular general election. This prompted Democrats to declare their primary a private affair, one in which only whites could vote. But the Supreme Court held, in *Smith v. Allwright* (1944), that to bar blacks from Democratic primaries in the South was in reality a violation of their right to vote guaranteed by the Fifteenth Amendment. Thus, the all–white, private primary was thwarted.

Residence and Registration Requirements. Blacks also were often kept from voting by the stringent residence and registration requirements of some states. But such requirements worked against others besides blacks. Young persons and other highly mobile groups, like migrant laborers, often could not meet residence requirements because of moves made for employment or schooling. Some critics have charged that elites conspired against such "undesirables" as students, blacks, and the working class because of fears of how these groups might vote if given the opportunity.

Reform of registration and residence requirements began with the Civil Rights Act of 1957, which authorized the attorney general to seek court injunctions against voting rights violations. More importantly, the act created a Civil Rights Commission to investigate voting rights violations and recommend appropriate legal remedies. The Civil Rights Act of 1960 went further and authorized courts to appoint referees to help blacks register to vote if the court found that discrimination was being practiced. This act also required that voting registrars keep records of voter registration applications.

Another major step was taken in 1965 when a voting rights act passed by Congress authorized the use of federal registrars in place of state officials where literacy tests had been used in the 1964 election and less than 50 percent of those eligible were registered or had voted in 1964. This act was renewed and expanded in the Voting Rights Acts of 1970 and 1975.

The Voting Rights Act of 1970 also dealt with the question of residency. It set a maximum residency requirement of thirty days for presidential elections. The Supreme Court's decision in *Dunn v. Blumstein* (1972) expanded the requirement for a "reasonable" registration deadline to all elections.

One problem created by the latter court verdict is the status of college students in a college community. While students can obviously meet the thirty–day residency requirement, some communities have balked at registering students, claiming they are not really residing in the community. The permanent residents obviously fear the election of students to important community government positions as has occured in Ann Arbor, Michigan, and Berkeley, California, two university communities.

Other Barriers.   The Voting Rights Acts of 1970, 1975, and 1982 eliminated two other subtle barriers to voting. The act first established uniform requirements for state laws which regulate absentee voting. This resulted in easier absentee balloting in many states. The 1975 act requires the use of bilingual ballots in areas of the country which have significant non–English–speaking populations. This increased the turnout among Hispanic-Americans in particular. The 1982 act simplified the process of proving voting rights violations by stating that a law or election procedure that results in discrimination is illegal even if its intent is not to discriminate.

By 1970, the major remaining legal barriers to universal suffrage were laws in forty-six states prohibiting voting by persons under twenty-one years of age. In Georgia and Kentucky, eighteen to twenty year olds were eligible to vote; nineteen and twenty year olds were eligible in Alaska; and twenty year olds were voting in Hawaii. Under a provision of the Voting Rights Act of 1970, Congress made all persons eighteen or older eligible to vote in local, state, and national elections. This action constituted the largest single expansion of the electorate since the women's suffrage amendment of 1920. The action of Congress was soon reversed by the courts, however. The Supreme Court held, in *Oregon v. Mitchell* (1970), that Congress could not lower the voting age for state or local elections. So a constitutional amendment was passed in a matter of months which made eighteen the minimum voting age for *all* elections. This amendment, the Constitution's Twenty-sixth, was ratified in 1971, so that the 1972 presidential contest could have involved up to twenty-five million new voters. Young Americans' response to this new opportunity, however, was less enthusiastic than anticipated, as we shall see further on in this chapter.

Conclusion. We have shown that numerous laws and court decisions have been made with the specific intent of expanding the electorate and voter participation. These are summarized in Table 3–1. Despite their good intent, however, these laws and decisions have not restored turnout rates to the lofty heights achieved in the 1870s.

Psychology and Voter Turnout

The authors of *The American Voter* established almost from the beginning of electoral research the existence of a strong link between psychology and turnout:

> We assume that the decision to vote, no less than the decision to vote for a given party, rests immediately on psychological forces. . . . Hence, our quest of understanding begins with an examination of motivational forces. . . . and will describe a number of psychological influences that affect the likelihood the individual will vote.[6]

Psychological motivation was found, in *The American Voter,* to spring from several forces: intensity of partisanship, perceived close-

Table 3-1
Law and Voter Turnout: A Summary

Year	Action	Significance
1870	15th Amendment	Prohibited voter discrimination because of race
1920	19th Amendment	Prohibited voter discrimination because of sex
1944	*Smith v. Allwright*	Prohibited all-white party primaries
1957	Civil Rights Act of 1957	Authorized Department of Justice to protect voting rights in the courts
1960	Civil Rights Act of 1960	Authorized courts to appoint referees to assist with voter registration
1961	23rd Amendment	Allowed District of Columbia residents to vote in presidential elections
1964	24th Amendment	Prohibited use of poll taxes in national elections
1965	Voting Rights Act of 1965	Suspended literacy tests; authorized federal voter registrars in 7 states
1966	*Harper v. Virginia State Board of Elections*	Prohibited poll taxes in any election
1970	Voting Rights Act of 1970	Lowered minimum voting age to 18 for federal elections; suspended state literacy tests; provided for uniform absentee voting rules
1971	26th Amendment	Lowered minimum voting age to 18 for all elections
1972	*Dunn v. Blumstein*	Shortened duration of residency requirements for voting
1975	Voting Rights Act of 1975	Extended more provisions of the 1970 Act; sent federal voter registrars to 10 additional states; provides for use of bilingual ballots
1982	Voting Rights Act of 1982	Extended provisions of the earlier 1970 and 1975 Acts; allowed private parties to prove a voting rights violation using a "results" test.

ness of an election, interest in the campaign, concern over the election outcome, sense of political efficacy, sense of personal efficacy, and sense of citizen duty. The general finding, therefore, was that intense psychological involvement in politics contributes to the likelihood of one's participation in elections. As data shown in Table 3–2 indicate, the relationship between one psychological factor, interest in the campaign, is as strong in recent years as it was in the 1950s.

Table 3-2
Interest in Campaign and Voter Turnout,
1956-1980

Degree of Interest in the Campaign	Voter Turnout						
	1956	1960	1964	1968	1972	1976	1980
High.............	87%	90%	88%	88%	86%	84%	79%
Medium.........	72	76	78	76	76	72	64
Low	58	38	63	52	51	47	35

Source: SRC/CPS Election Studies

Later research has shown that, as a general rule, turnout is linked to the salience which a particular election holds for the public. Important research on this theme was conducted by M. Kent Jennings and Harmon Zeigler. They found that national government affairs are more salient to most people than state or local government affairs.[7] This accounts for the persistent finding that turnout is higher in national elections than in either state or local elections. Of course the greater attention given by the news media to national elections and the more extensive use of the media in such campaigns may spur the greater salience of national elections.

Another aspect of the influence of salience is seen in turnout for different types of national elections. As we mentioned above, national elections have the highest turnout. But, as shown in Figure 3–2, turnout for presidential elections consistently exceeds turnout for nationwide congressional elections in off years (i.e., when we are not electing a president). Going further in our comparison of presidential and congressional elections, we should point out that even in years when we do elect a president, congressional election turnout is still lower. This phenomenon is known as *roll–off*. It occurs when people mark a ballot for a top office, like president, but do not bother to vote for lower offices such as congressional and legislative seats.

Figure 3-2
Voting Turnout in Elections for President and
House of Representatives, 1952-1982

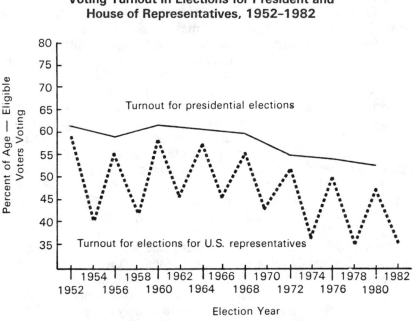

Source: U.S. Bureau of the Census, *Statistical Abstract of the United States: 1978*, Table No. 835, p. 520. 1978 data obtained from U.S. Department of Commerce.

Psychological factors are thought to account for the lower turnout in party primaries than in the general election (except in one–party–dominant states like those in the South). A longitudinal test of this hypothesis by Bone and Ranney, using data from 1962 and 1972, shows that "turnout in contested primary elections for governor and United States senator . . . was less than half as large as that in ensuing general elections."[8] Ranney also had shown previously that in presidential primaries turnout generally runs about half to two thirds of that in the general election which follows.[9] Bone and Ranney believe that general elections inspire greater turnout because voters see candidates of their own party as the "good guys" doing battle with the "bad guys," nominees of the other party. Primaries lack such a stimulus and are therefore uninspiring, or maybe even confusing and ambiguous in the choices they offer.

Three aspects of the relationship between psychology and turnout are not fully understood and pose dilemmas for researchers studying them. The first dilemma derives from the debate over the utility of voting. This area of concern was stimulated by Anthony Downs's suggestion that voting or nonvoting should be considered in terms of its rationality.[10] Rational voting would imply, in Downs's view, that the benefits of voting outweigh the costs of voting. He suggested that voting is, in many instances, irrational because it takes more time and effort than it is worth. Unless one is convinced that one's own vote will alter the election outcome, the effort made to vote is essentially foolhardy. But, subsequent research points out that voting may be seen as rational because not voting may cause one to feel guilt or neglect of citizen duty, or to experience various other psychological trauma.[11] Future research on turnout will have to consider further the question of rationality in voting.

Another dilemma of political scientists studying turnout involves the relation of citizens' evaluations of government to the act of voting. For example, does a positive orientation toward government inspire one to vote or not? From one perspective, a satisfied citizen may feel that it is unnecessary to vote because "things are already going so well" with government. But intuition and research tells us that a low turnout does not always mean that the citizenry is happy with government. In fact, low turnouts are often interpreted as symptomatic of deeply felt hostility toward or disappointment with government. The dilemma is whether apathy stems from satisfaction or dissatisfaction with government, and whether political activism indicates pride in government or efforts to "throw the bums out." This is indeed an extremely complex research problem and one which we will deal with in the final two chapters.

The third dilemma concerning psychology and turnout is primarily a theoretical issue. Is our system of government affected if people choose not to participate in elections? As we mentioned in Chapter 1, Bernard Berelson has expressed the sentiment that the system might collapse under pressure if everyone decided to become political activists.[12] Jack Walker, on the other hand, has countered that the system suffers if people stay away from the polls.[13] Voting and other participation integrates the participant into the system, he believes. While the argument may be valid that a voter cannot change the course of public affairs with one vote, continued voting over time can and does have a cumulative impact which benefits the voter, Walker argues.

These dilemmas illustrate a point we made at the beginning of this book: Despite our extensive knowledge of electoral behavior, there are many important and interesting, but as yet unresolved, questions about it.

Personal Characteristics and Turnout

The authors of *The American Voter* established strong linkages between certain demographic characteristics and electoral turnout. And most of these linkages continue to exist, even if not as strongly, down to the present time, as Table 3-3 shows. The characteristics listed in the table should only be viewed as a rough guide to some personal factors which affect turnout.

Table 3-3
Personal Characteristics and Voter Turnout

Higher Turnout	Lower Turnout
Strong partisans	Weak partisans and independents
Republicans	Democrats
College graduates	Less than eight years of school
Annual income above $25,000	Annual income below $7,500
Professional and technical workers	Unskilled laborers and unemployed
Persons 45–70 years old	Persons 18–24 years old
White persons	Nonwhite persons
Non–Southerners	Southerners
Jews	Protestants and Catholics

Some of these characteristics should not be viewed as causally related to turnout. For example, Republicans are more likely to vote than Democrats not because they are Republicans, but rather because Republicans tend to be disproportionately drawn from high–turnout groups like college graduates and high–income persons. The same logic may apply to other categories like religion and race.

Research since *The American Voter* shows interesting changes in the voting habits of three groups: (1) blacks, (2) women, and (3) the young.

Turnout among Blacks. There are two facets of change in blacks'
voting turnout before 1982 worth noting. First as shown in Table 3–4,
in the North and West black electoral participation declined dramati-

Table 3–4
Reported Voter Turnout Among Blacks,
By Region, 1964–1982

	North & West		South	
	Presidential	Congressional	Presidential	Congressional
1964....	72%		44%	
1966....		52%		33%
1968....	65		52	
1970....		51		37
1972....	57		48	
1974....		38		30
1976....	52		46	
1978....		41		33
1980....	53		48	
1982....		48		38

Source: U.S. Bureau of the Census, *Current Population Reports,* Series P–20, No.
370; press release, U.S. Bureau of the Census, April 18, 1983.

Table 3–5
Reported Voter Turnout, By Race, 1964–1982

Year	Black Turnout	White Turnout	Difference
1964	58.5%	70.7%	12.2%
1966	41.7	57.0	15.3
1968	57.6	69.1	11.5
1970	43.5	56.0	12.5
1972	52.1	64.5	12.4
1974	33.8	46.3	12.5
1976	48.7	60.9	12.2
1978	37.2	47.3	10.1
1980	50.5	60.9	10.4
1982	43.0	49.9	6.9

Source: U.S. Bureau of the Census, *Current Population Reports,* Series P–20, No.
370; press release, U.S. Bureau of the Census, April 18, 1983.

cally between 1964 and 1976 before leveling out in 1980 at 53 percent. In the South, there was an upward spurt in black voting in 1968 and 1970. However, between 1970 and 1982, voting turnout among Southern blacks declined, hovering several points below 50 percent in presidential elections. A second and perhaps more important observation about longitudinal change in black turnout can be made by comparing black and white turnout over the past two decades. As shown in Table 3–5, the gap between black and white voting, while marginally smaller than it was in 1964, persisted at a surprisingly high level, about 10 percent until 1982. This must have been very discouraging to those who worked so hard to increase black input into the electoral decision-making process, especially in the South. Even intense federal efforts to sponsor black voter registration have failed to achieve the desired results. Black registration rates have fallen since 1968 and remain about six points below white registration.

Obviously legal reform alone, such as that summarized in Table 3–1, may not be sufficient to bring about resolution of the problem of lower black turnout levels. Evidence of change that may reflect such reform, however, is the dramatic increase in the numbers of black elected officials, particularly in the South.[14] And perhaps more encouraging was the sudden increase in black turnout in the 1982 congressional elections and several 1983 mayoral contests. As shown in Table 3–5, black turnout in 1982 jumped to 43 percent, nearly 6 percent higher than black turnout in the last congressional election, and only 6.9 percentage points lower than white turnout. Considering that black turnout had always been 10 points lower than white turnout before this election, the events of 1982 were very significant. Table 3–4 shows that black turnout in 1982 increased in the South and the rest of the nation. Harold Washington's controversial election as mayor of Chicago in 1983 benefitted from the trend of upward black turnout. In Chicago, more than 60 percent of blacks of voting age turned out to vote, most for Harold Washington. Whether this surge in turnout will continue remains to be seen.

Turnout among Women. The trend in turnout among women exhibits more significant change. The turnout rate among women, once well below that of men, is now virtually identical (see Table 3–6). In his analysis of sex and turnout data from the 1972 SRC/CPS election study, Gerald Pomper made the following additional observations about women's turnout:

Table 3-6
Reported Voter Turnout, By Sex, 1964-1982

Year	Males	Females	Difference
1964	71.9%	67.0	4.9%
1966	58.2	53.0	5.2
1968	69.8	66.0	3.8
1970	56.8	52.7	4.1
1972	64.1	62.0	2.1
1974	46.2	43.4	2.8
1976	59.6	58.8	0.8
1978	46.6	45.3	1.3
1980	59.1	59.4	0.3
1982	48.7	48.4	0.3

Source: U.S. Bureau of the Census, *Current Population Reports,* Series P-20, Nos. 143, 174, 192, 228, 253, 293, 332, and 370; press release, U.S. Bureau of the Census, April 18, 1983.

1. Lower female participation is evident only among older and less-educated white Southerners.
2. Lower female voting in the South is a manifestation of a regional culture.
3. Female voting is depressed by responsibilities for the care of young children.[15]

Data from the 1980 Census Bureau election study indicate further that female turnout runs well ahead of male turnout in the West, particularly among blacks and Hispanics, and among Southern blacks. But as Pomper found in 1972, turnout among older white Southern women continues to lag behind that of their male counterparts. Nevertheless, most women apparently have now been socialized as a group to realize fully the important role of voting in a democracy. If such a socialization process has occurred, we can expect overall turnout among women to equal turnout among males in future elections even if there are a few regional and ethnic variations such as those described above.

Age-Related Turnout. Philip Converse, one of the authors of *The American Voter,* analyzed the Michigan studies of the 1952 and 1956 elections and came to two conclusions regarding age and turnout. First, he noted the existence of a *political life cycle* in which persons turn out more frequently for elections as they get older (up to a certain age, sixty to sixty-five, when turnout decreases).[16] This cycle is depicted in Figure

3-3 using 1980 data. The second observation, which also can be seen in Figure 3-3, is that young persons and very old persons also vote proportionately less in off-year congressional elections.

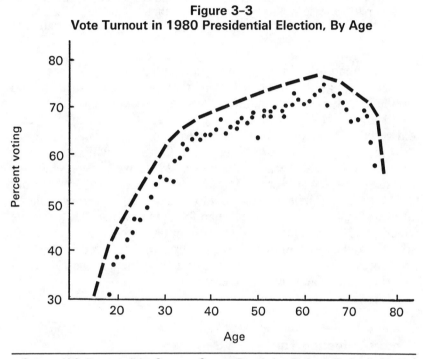

Figure 3-3
Vote Turnout in 1980 Presidential Election, By Age

Source: U.S. Bureau of the Census, *Current Population Reports,* Series P–20, No. 370.

Converse's life cycle notion has been widely accepted. It makes sense. Persons in their middle years, the years in which they are most affected by society and politics, are most likely to vote. Young persons may not vote because of an absence of social responsibilities, or because of apathy. Old persons may be physically infirm and cannot vote or live alone and do not receive social reinforcement from friends or family to vote.

But some studies indicate that young persons who entered the electorate in the late 1960s and 1970s may not be participating according to the pattern which past experience would suggest. V. Lance Tarrance notes a "pattern of decreasing turnout among successively younger birth cohorts." Further, he states:

> The major conclusion is that younger age cohorts have matured in a period of lowered partisan intensity and reduced community pressures to engage in political activity, and that "cohort effects of historical periods are now known to be important sources of variation in the voting decision."[17]

Such a trend—declining youth turnout with continued nonparticipation after aging—was not expected by those who campaigned so hard for the Twenty-sixth Amendment. This trend seemed to continue into 1980, when only 36 percent of all persons eighteen to twenty-one years old voted. If these persons follow the pattern of those who were eighteen to twenty-one in 1972, only about 33 percent will vote in their second presidential election, the one in 1984. We can guess at this because persons who were eighteen to twenty-one in 1972 turned out at 48.3 percent. But in 1976 only about 45.6 percent of their age cohorts turned out, about 3 percent less than four years earlier. But first–time voters in 1976 were more likely to vote in their second election, 1980, so perhaps the problem trend identified by Tarrance is ending. Perhaps the process of aging will eventually cause new voters of the 1960s and 1970s to vote at an expected rate.

Factors Affecting Turnout: A Summary

Critics of the American electorate are often vocal in berating citizens for not voting in greater numbers than we have found. They point out that citizens of European democracies have much greater turnout rates than is the case in America.

Some political scientists have countered that when certain factors are taken into account, turnout in American elections does not look so bad. For example, one innovative and creative study of the 1960 presidential election concludes that "80 to 85 percent of those legally eligible and physically able to vote did so."[18] The only problem in applying that study to the 1970s is that a greater proportion of the electorate is now legally eligible to vote. When the few remaining legal and physical considerations are taken into account, Bone and Ranney find that only about 66 percent of the citizenry voted in 1972.[19] So we must conclude that turnout among those legally and physically eligible to vote has declined more than is evident in reported turnout figures available from the Census Bureau and SRC/CPS.

The reasons behind the overall downward trend of American turnout rates are not easily determined. Converse notes that "all attitudinal factors for nonvoting were less frequent than legal (nonregistration) or personal (ill health, flat tire, etc.) reasons" during the 1950s.[20] And, as Converse's data demonstrate in Table 3-7, over twice as many persons cited personal rather than attitudinal reasons for not voting in the 1952 and 1956 elections. More recent data from 1972 through 1980 seem to bear out the same conclusion today. People still report more often than any other reason that they simply cannot get to the polls because of health, transportation, or other problems. Of course, these responses may be *post hoc* excuses which belie apathy or lack of concern about politics, but we cannot be sure.

Data reported on reasons for nonregistration (Table 3-8) are also revealing of the excuses for nonparticipation. From 1970 to 1980 there was a drop in the frequency of cases where persons blame their actions on residency requirements. This makes sense when one considers the reform in residency requirements over the same period. The interesting increase over this period is in the numbers of persons who have vague reasons or no reasons for not being registered. Of course, rational justifications are difficult to come by in our reasonably open registration system.

But perhaps our system of voting and registration should be made even more open. President Carter believed so. In 1977 he called for the elimination of all laws which require citizens to register before election day. Under his proposal voters could register when they voted. Such reform has been tried in some states, and it seems to be helpful in increasing turnout.[21]

Finally, some observers still contend that turnout would be improved if the electorate had a better attitude toward government and elections. This consideration will be broached in the final two chapters.

OTHER FORMS OF PARTICIPATION

There have been two alternative explanations of political participation. One, primarily identified with Lester Milbraith's research, sug-

Table 3-7

Reported Reason for Not Voting, Registered Voters Only, 1952–1980

Reason for not voting	1952–56	1972	1974	1976	1978	1980
Health problem; no transportation; out of town; other unavoidable reason	68%	48%	45%	53%	44%	42%
Not interested; apathetic; dislike politics, candidates, etc.	32	27	32	23	25	27
Other reason or reason not reported	—*	25	23	24	31	31
	100%	100%	100%	100%	100%	100%

*This category was not included in the 1952–56 report. This has the result of inflating the other two categories reported in 1952–56.

Source: 1952–56 data from Philip E. Converse with Richard Niemi, "Non-Voting Among Young Adults in the United States," in *Political Parties and Political Behavior* (2d ed.), eds. W. J. Crotty, D. M. Freeman and D. S. Gatlin (Boston: Allyn & Bacon, 1971); 1972–80 data from U.S. Bureau of the Census, *Current Population Reports*, Series P-20, Nos. 253, 293, 322, and 370.

Table 3–8
Reported Reason for Not Registering to Vote, 1970–1980

Reason Not Registered	Percentage of Those Not Registered					
	1970	1972	1974	1976	1978	1980
Unable to Register						
Not a citizen.............	9%	11%	9%	11%	11%	15%
Did not meet residence requirement.........	14	6	4	3	*	*
Other unable, including.............	12	12	24	18	25	29
Recent move, didn't get around to it						
No transportation						
Didn't know where to register						
Physical disability						
Not Interested	50	43	37	29	38	33
Other Reason	11	23	21	35	17	15
Don't Know or Reason Not Reported.........	4	5	5	4	9	8
	100%	100%	100%	100%	100%	100%

*Categories not reported separately in Census data.
Source: U.S. Bureau of the Census, Current Population Reports, Series P–20, Nos. 192, 228, 253, 293, 322, and 370.

gests that participation is cumulative and that different forms of participation can be ranked according to difficulty.[22] For example, voting is relatively easy to do when compared with attending a campaign rally. Thus, persons who attend a rally should also vote.

A second concept of participation is associated with the work of Sidney Verba and Norman Nie, who conclude that citizens have certain participation specialties.[23] For example, some people do not vote but instead seek to contact public officials in person or with letters. Other persons concentrate on group activities, like party work. Some persons may have several specialties, but many have only one—voting. Verba and Nie estimate that about 21 percent of the populace limits its participation to the simple act of voting. More importantly, they found that 22 percent of the electorate specializes in doing absolutely nothing. These are the "inactives."

Americans, like other citizens of developed democracies, engage in few acts of political participation other than voting. This has been shown repeatedly in the SRC-CPS's reports of public participation in such acts as going to a political rally or meeting, working for a party or candidate, wearing a campaign button or putting a campaign sticker on one's car, belonging to a political club, or contributing money to a party or candidate. Table 3–9 shows that none of these acts involves more than 1 American in 5. While no trend of decreasing participation is evident in these less common forms of participation, presidential voting turnouts have been falling since 1964, when reported turnout was 79 percent (actual turnout in 1964 was 62 percent), to 1980, when reported turnout was 71 percent (actual turnout was 53 percent). These data also provide support for the cumulative *and* the specialization theories of individual political participation as discussed above.

VOTING TURNOUT IN THE STATES

There is often the temptation, for purposes of brevity and simplicity, to discuss only the national scope of declining participation in presidential elections. And, furthermore, we often overlook related trends in voting for state and local offices. Such oversights can be explained in part by the fact that national opinion surveys produce samples which usually are too small to say much about regional or state differences in any of the patterns we have been discussing. But we do have actual

Table 3-9
Political Participation: 1952–1980

Political Activity	1952	1956	1960	1964	1968	1972	1976	1980
Worked for party or candidate	3%	3%	6%	5%	6%	5%	4%	4%
Attended rallies or meetings...........	7	7	8	9	9	9	6	8
Tried to persuade others how to vote...........	27	28	33	32	33	32	37	36
Wore campaign button, displayed bumper sticker	—	16	21	16	15	14	8	7
Belonged to political club or organization	2	3	3	4	3	—	—	3
Contributed money to campaign	4	10	12	11	9	10	9	6
Voted (reported turnout, *not* actual turnout)	73	73	74	79	76	73	72	71
Number responding...........	1,742	1,762	1,829	1,450	1,351	2,285	2,868.5*	1,407

*Weighted sample.
Source: SRC/CPS Election Studies.

election turnout data for each of the states across time. These data include turnout figures for presidential elections, off-year congressional elections that fall in even-numbered years when presidents are not elected, and gubernatorial elections, some of which are held in even years and some of which are held in odd-numbered years when we are electing neither a president nor a congress.

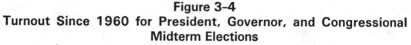

Figure 3-4
Turnout Since 1960 for President, Governor, and Congressional Midterm Elections

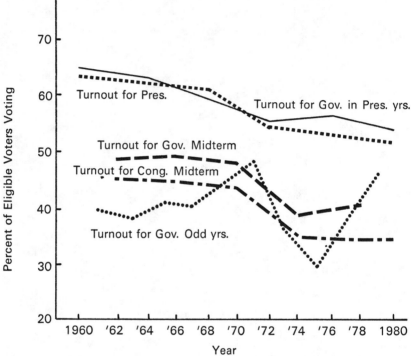

Turnout trends for each of these types of elections are depicted in Figure 3-4. (The percentages reported in the figure represent actual turnout and were calculated by dividing the total number of votes cast in all states holding each respective type of election by the total number of eligible voters in those states.) We can see that there has been a steady decline in turnout across all types of elections, except for the relatively few gubernatorial elections which are held in odd–numbered years. Turnout in those elections declined from 1971 to 1975, but has risen steadily ever since. While the percentage turnout for presidential elections declined 11.5 points between 1960 and 1980, turnout in off–year congressional elections and gubernatorial elections held with presidential elections each declined 10.2 points and turnout in off–year gubernatorial elections was off 7.8 points. Thus, with the exception of the odd–year contests, the drop–off in turnout over the last two decades has similarly touched every type of election.

The overall decline in turnout has varied across the states, however, as is shown in Figure 3–5. The map shows average declines in turnout over all gubernatorial, off–year congressional and presidential elections. Nineteen states in a belt extending from New England to Washington and California have experienced a decline of at least .9 percent each year on average for the three elections. This represents a decline of more than 18 percent for the entire 1960–1980 period. Eight states, all in the South, have experienced an increase in turnout during this period. This represents an overall increase of about 8 percent since 1960. Turnout in the other states has remained relatively stable. Accounting for these patterns of change is all but impossible given the fact that we do not have opinion surveys for each of the separate states.

A TREND ASSESSMENT: POLITICAL PARTICIPATION

In this analysis we will consider trends in political participation as a variable in the changing nature of the American voter. Specifically, we will seek to assess whether some eligible voters do not participate in the political life of our nation because they are disenchanted by the options afforded by the two major political parties or, alternatively, because they are increasingly sophisticated in the evaluation of candidates and find no one espousing the issues or ideological positions they favor. But before we consider such relationships and whether there has been a change over time, we must consider the nature of political participation.

As we have noted, few Americans engage in political activity other than voting, even in the peak periods of presidential election years. It has been an issue of mild concern in political science whether those who engage in the more unusual forms of political participation also

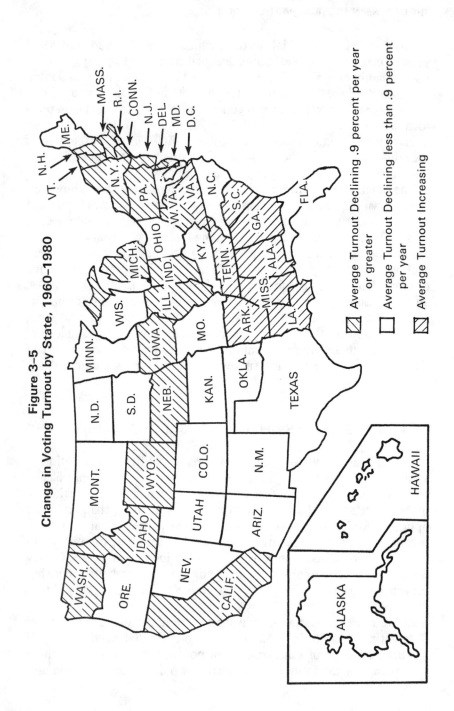

Figure 3-5
Change in Voting Turnout by State, 1960–1980

Average Turnout Declining .9 percent per year or greater

Average Turnout Declining less than .9 percent per year

Average Turnout Increasing

participate in the more common forms, such as voting.[24] Because we felt it would be more informative to have a measure of political participation which did more than divide people as to whether or not they voted, we attempted to include in our measure whether the person also contributed money to a candidate, attended political rallies or meetings, wore a campaign button, or belonged to a political club. This effort, however, was unsuccessful. Some of the SRC/CPS surveys on which we based our analysis omitted some questions on participation; others found one or more acts of participation unrelated to other acts, and probably most important, most people fell either within the "voted–only" category or the "did not participate at all" category. The measure of political participation used in this book is thus a simple dichotomy of those who voted for president in a specific election versus those that did not.

Typically about one American in four reports that he or she did not vote for president. Nonparticipation has varied little, according to the reports of the SRC/CPS surveys. Across the years reported nonparticipation or nonvoting is: 1952, 27 percent; 1956, 27 percent; 1960, 26 percent; 1964, 21 percent; 1968, 24 percent; 1972, 27 percent; 1976, 28 percent; and 1980, 29 percent. While the peak of participation was the 1964 election, when 78 percent of those interviewed reported they voted for president, the elections in the 1950s and those in the 1970s still show nearly identical rates of participation. The small rise in participation until 1964 and subsequent decline closely parallels the voting turnout reported by the Bureau of Census, but at a somewhat higher level of voting. This may be overreporting, due to simple lying to impress the interviewer, or it may be a real increase in participation by those who were stimulated to vote by having been interviewed during the campaign.[25] This is fascinating but beyond the scope of this test.

Table 3–10 shows the percentage of participants (voters) who have achieved the six different levels of sophistication in candidate evaluations (as explained in Chapter 2). In 1952, only 17 percent of all participants achieved an issue–oriented level of candidate evaluation, while 68 percent of all participants achieved only an image rating for their candidate evaluation. By contrast, at the highpoint of issue evaluation, 1972, nearly half of all voters (48 percent) mentioned issues in their evaluations of the candidates. This represents nearly a tripling of issue-evaluating voters. The low point of the less sophisticated image evaluation came in 1980 when one voter in five differentiated between the candidates solely in terms of superficial image differences, such as "I

Table 3-10
Candidate Evaluations Among American Voters

Percentage of Respondents Using Various
Types of Candidate Evaluations

	Ideologue	Issue Oriented	Group Benefit	Partisan	Image	No Content	Number
1952..	1%	17%	4%	1%	68%	10%	1,704
1956..	1	19	6	—	68	6	1,761
1960..	2	22	5	—	65	7	1,103
1964..	6	37	4	—	47	6	1,440
1968..	4	24	4	20	39	9	1,319
1972..	9	48	6	5	28	5	1,118
1976..	8	38	9	14	26	3	1,600
1980..	13	50	3	6	19	9	1,407

Source: SRC/CPS Election Studies.

like him" or "I like his smile." Certainly, participants in presidential elections show a marked improvement in their evaluation of the presidential candidates.

Table 3-11 presents the same data but from a different perspective. The percentage of each type of candidate evaluators who voted is shown for each election. No change is evident across the years. Ideological evaluators, those using concepts such as liberal or conservative, consistently prove the most participant of all citizens. Those with no-content evaluations, which means they had nothing to say in evaluating either candidate, prove far and away least likely to participate; an average of 48 percent report they did vote. Every group shows a high point of participation in the early 1960s but returns to 1950 levels or lower in the 1970s.

Our main concern is with the issue-oriented evaluators. Since issue-oriented citizens have been increasingly common among voters (Table 3-10), and since issue-oriented evaluators show no change in participation which is not also notable among other evaluators (Table 3-11), it seems that there are just more issue-oriented evaluators and that this change is unrelated to the act of voting. It may well be that participation has been declining since the 1960s and that issues play an increasingly important part in the candidate evaluations given by the general public, but these same issue evaluations are not contributing to the decline of political participation.

Table 3–11
Percentage of Different Types of
Candidate Evaluators Voting

	Type of Candidate Evaluation						
	Ideologue	Issue Oriented	Group Benefit	Partisan	Image	No Content	Number
1952..	87%	76%	63%	71%	79%	48%	1,704
1956..	87	72	73	—	78	42	1,761
1960..	100	87	84	—	85	50	1,103
1964..	81	80	69	75	81	51	1,440
1968..	93	79	64	77	79	54	1,319
1972..	87	73	79	61	72	43	1,118
1976..	77	74	70	72	67	33	1,600
1980..	87	74	60	80	68	53	1,407

Source: SRC/CPS Election Studies.

Partisanship and Participation

Inasmuch as somewhat fewer persons are now identifying with one of the major political parties and voting has declined in presidential elections since the 1960s by better than 10 percent, could it be the independents who are increasingly choosing not to vote? As we have seen, the independent in early studies of voting proved marginally more uninterested in the campaign and marginally less likely to vote. Table 3–12 confirms this pattern of lower turnout by independents across all presidential elections since 1952.

A nearly consistent pattern is evident, as the strong partisans prove most participant, followed by the weak partisans (including those independents who admit to be leaning toward one of the parties), and finally the independents. But the pattern has been one of sharply declining participation by independents (except for a small rebound in 1980), mild decline among weak partisans evident only in 1976, and little change among strong partisans. While in the 1950s strong partisans were marginally more likely to vote, and weak partisans and independents differed little in their voting turnout, the pattern in the 1970s is one of sharply declining participation as the analysis moves from strong partisans to weak partisans to independents.

The significance of nonparticipation by independents should not be exaggerated. Pure independents, even in 1980, constituted only a small percentage of the total electorate (12 percent). More significant is the

Table 3–12
Percentage of Persons of
Differing Partisan Commitments Voting
(Numbers in Parentheses)

	Strong Partisans	Weak Partisans and Leaning Independents	Independents (not leaning)
1952	82%	73%	72%
	(566)	(896)	(79)
1956	80	73	75
	(626)	(908)	(155)
1960	87	82	75
	(410)	(549)	(98)
1964	84	77	59
	(548)	(764)	(105)
1968	83	75	63
	(398)	(767)	(134)
1972	82	72	51
	(572)	(1395)	(281)
1976	85	68	50
	(547)	(1419)	(331)
1980	85	71	55
	(372)	(829)	(176)

Source: SRC/CPS Election Studies.

fact that 79 percent of all citizens who failed to vote for president in 1980 were partisans. Nonvoting among partisans affect more people and thus demands more attention.

Conclusions

Independents increasingly fail to vote. Those evaluating candidates in terms of issues and ideological concepts persist in being the most likely to vote. Thus increasing independence from political parties has contributed to declining participation, but the improvement in candidate evaluation within the electorate has had no effect, neither increasing nor decreasing participation. As we have pointed out previously, numerous researchers have suggested that the quality of candidate evaluations plays a crucial role in the effort to tie together the various trends we have introduced thus far in our explanation of American political behavior. The fact that we have found no significant relationship between public evaluation of presidential candidates and trends in partisanship, defection from party, and political participation suggests that new explanations of American voting behavior are in order. But before suggesting our own alternative considerations on behavior of the electorate, we should add the facts on the relationships between the four variables thus far considered—(1) defection from party identification, (2) nature of independency, (3) quality of candidate evaluation and (4) participation—and the subject of the next chapter, political distrust and alienation.

NOTES

1. Hugh A. Bone and Austin Ranney, *Politics and Voters,* 4th ed. (New York: McGraw-Hill, 1976), p. 35. For further discussion of misreporting of voting see Michael W. Traugott and John P. Katosh, "Response Validity in Surveys of Voting Behavior," *Public Opinion Quarterly* 45 (Winter, 1981).

2. Bone and Ranney, *Politics and Voters,* p. 4.

3. Philip E. Converse, "Change in the American Electorate," in *The Human Meaning of Social Change,* eds. Angus Campbell and Philip E. Converse (New York: Russell Sage Foundation, 1972): Jerrold D. Rusk, "The Effect of the Australian Ballot Reform on Split Ticket Voting: 1876-1908," *American Political Science Review* 64 (December 1970); Walter Dean Burnham, "The Changing Shape of the American Political Universe," *American Political Science Review* 59 (March 1965).

4. Converse, "Change in American Electorate," p. 281 ff.

5. Jack C. Plano and Milton Greenberg, *The American Political Dictionary* (Hinsdale, Ill.: Dryden Press, 1976), p. 125.

6. Angus Campbell et al., *The American Voter* (Chicago: University of Chicago Press, 1960), p. 90.

7. M. Kent Jennings and Harmon Zeigler, "The Salience of American State Politics," *American Political Science Review* 64 (June 1970): 523-35.

8. Bone and Ranney, *Politics and Voters,* pp. 32-33.

9. Austin Ranney, "Turnout and Representation in Presidential Primary Elections," *American Political Science Review* 66 (March 1972).

10. Anthony Downs, *An Economic Theory of Democracy* (New York: Harper, 1957).

11. William H. Riker and Peter C. Ordershook, "A Theory of the Calculus of Voting," *American Political Science Review* 62 (March 1968): 25-42; Rich-

ard G. Niemi and Herbert F. Weisberg, *Controversies in American Voting Behavior* (San Francisco: W. H. Freeman, 1976), p. 27.

12. Bernard R. Berelson, Paul F. Lazarsfeld, and William N. McPhee, *Voting* (Chicago: University of Chicago Press, 1954), Chap. 14.

13. Jack L. Walker, "A Critique of the Elitist Theory of Democracy," *American Political Science Review* 60 (June 1966): 285–95.

14. Lucius J. Barker and Jesse J. McCorry, Jr., report that there are over 3,500 elected black officials today, the majority of whom reside in the South, in *Black Americans and the Political System* (Cambridge; Mass.: Winthrop Publishers, 1976), pp. 9, 113–20.

15. Gerald M. Pomper, *Voters' Choice: Varieties of American Electoral Behavior* (New York: Dodd, Mead & Co., 1975), p. 88.

16. Philip E. Converse with Richard Niemi, "Non-voting among Young Adults in the United States," in *Political Parties and Political Behavior* (2nd ed., ed. William J. Crotty, D. M. Freeman, and D. S. Gatlin (Boston: Allyn & Bacon, 1971), pp. 443–66.

17. V. Lance Tarrance, "The Vanishing Voter: A Look at Non–Voting as a Purposive Act," in *Voters, Primaries and Parties,* eds. Jonathan Moore and Albert C. Pierce (Cambridge, Mass.: Harvard University Institute of Politics, 1976), p. 12.

18. William G. Andrews, "American Voting Participation," *The Western Political Quarterly* 19 (1966): 630–39.

19. Bone and Ranney, *Politics and Voters,* p. 36.

20. Converse with Niemi, "Non–voting among Young Adults," p. 455.

21. Stanley Kelley, Jr., et al., "Registration and Voting: Putting First Things First," *American Political Science Review* 61 (June 1967): 359–77; Raymond E. Wolfinger and Steven J. Rosenstone, *Who Votes?* (New Haven: Yale, 1980).

22. Lester W. Milbraith and M. L. Goel, *Political Participation,* 2d ed. (Chicago: Rand McNally, 1977).

23. Sidney Verba and Norman H. Nie, *Participation in America* (New York: Harper & Row, 1972).

24. For a brief description of these issues, see Milbraith and Goel, *Political Participation,* p. 12.

25. Michael Traugott and John Katosh, "Response Validity in Surveys of Voting Behavior," *Public Opinion Quarterly* 43 (Fall, 1979): 359–77.

Berry's World

"Put me down as having a deeply felt sense of powerlessness and disengagement, which has led to a profound crisis of confidence."

CHAPTER 4

The Decline in Political Trust

Political scientists have seen Americans move from an attitude of benign affection for government during the 1950s and early 1960s to a state of apparent distrust, lack of confidence, and alienation in the 1970s and 1980s. *The American Voter,* dating from the period of trust in government, gave scant attention in its conceptualizations to distrust, protests, or any form of violent political behavior. Many contemporary observers see the growth of distrust as a refutation of the American Voter model introduced in Chapter 1.

In order to evaluate this trend, we must consider the historical context of declining trust or increasing alienation. The Korean War and the tumultuous McCarthy hearings on Communists in America had largely faded in the public's memory at the time of the 1956 presidential election. Our nation was at peace with the world, and the Cold War had not begun to heat up as it eventually did in the 1960s. Because of the relative calm of this period, Americans probably gave less thought to government and political issues. And those thoughts they did maintain were essentially positive. The notion of an alienated, politically estranged citizenry was so remote that it was not until the 1958 election survey that Michigan's Survey Research Center asked respondents to express positive or negative statements about government officials. Nowhere in *The American Voter,* that period's most comprehensive document on American political behavior, was there mention of any negative sentiment about government among the masses.

Early studies of political socialization discovered that children, like adults, were happy with government and politics during the late 1950s and early 1960s. It was difficult during this period to find a child or adolescent who would express any doubt about the goodness or greatness of the president. One study demonstrated that American children felt that leaders were more trustworthy and better people than were their own parents.[1]

Perhaps one of the most important developments to grow out of these early studies of children's behavior was a comprehensive theory of the concept of political support. David Easton developed a *systems theory* of political life in which he hypothesized that Americans have two types of support.[2] The first type of support is based on evaluations of political authorities and how they perform. Easton referred to individuals' evaluations of leaders and their policies as *specific support* and suggested that there is also a second type of support, which he called *diffuse support*. This second type has little to do with the actions of specific political authorities. Instead it focuses on the acceptance or rejection of the basic aspects of the whole political system. Easton differentiates the concepts of diffuse and specific support by stating that the former "represents more enduring bonds and thereby makes it possible for members to oppose the incumbents of offices and yet retain respect for the offices themselves, for the way in which they are ordered, and for the community of which they are a part." Specific support is "directed to the perceived decisions, policies, actions, utterances or the general style of . . . authorities."[3]

While Easton considered the maintenance of specific support to be important, he considered the existence of diffuse support to be absolutely necessary. The consequences of a failure to generate diffuse support are catastrophic, according to Easton, because if "the input of support falls below minimum, the persistence of any kind of system will be endangered. A system will finally succumb unless it adopts measures to cope with the stress."[4]

Easton and other scholars agree on the potential impact of low levels of support and concomitant high levels of alienation. As William Flanigan and Nancy Zingale have stated, "at a minimum, demands for social and political change will be widespread."[5] Edward Muller suggests more directly that when low levels of political trust are combined with a high degree of belief in effectiveness of violent protests, political violence may well occur.[6]

Perhaps Arthur Miller best sums up the concerns about trust in government with these words:

A democratic political system cannot survive for long without the support of a majority of its citizens. When such support wanes, underlying discontent is the necessary result and the potential for revolutionary alteration of the political and social system is enhanced. . . . when dissatisfaction with the existing situation leads to pervasive distrust of government . . . flexibility [of the system] is greatly curtailed, thereby increasing the potential for radical change.[7]

With this basis of understanding for the theoretical implications of political support, we will examine carefully the meaning of terms which have been used to describe various dimensions of political support.

THE MEANING OF ALIENATION

Political alienation and malaise have become perhaps two of the most overworked terms in political science and political news coverage. We are besieged with reports of one poll or another which indicate that Americans are alienated from their leaders. Indeed, as we will show further on in this chapter, there is evidence that alienation from government and other social institutions has become one of the most significant changes among Americans. But before looking at the substance of change in the realm of political alienation, we must precisely define the term as it is used by political scientists.

While the word *alienation* has taken on numerous meanings throughout history, it has usually implied that there is a separation between two things. The term was probably first used by Christian philosophers to indicate a separation between mankind and God. Philosophers like Jean Jacques Rousseau and Karl Marx took the concept of alienation into other realms. For example, Rousseau used the concept to describe what he saw as a separation between mankind and the "natural state." Karl Marx came to believe that alienation "meant the separation of man from his humanness and from his natural social development." Both Rousseau and Marx, like other philosophers who have examined the concept of alienation, believed that humans' separation from something else was prompted by conditions in the society in which mankind exists.

Some students of philosophy argue that social scientists have overused the term *alienation* and have applied it in some instances inappropriately. Almost all scholars agree, however, that there are numerous acceptable meanings of the term. We will say, therefore that alienation is a *multidimensional concept*. The multidimensionality of alienation comes from defining the nature of the separation which is being described. Alienation also takes on a multidimensional character in that humans' separation may be from any of a multiplicity of objects, like society, self, or government. Thus, to understand alienation fully, we must identify both the type of separation *and* the object or objects from which this separation is experienced.

TYPES OF ALIENATION

There are at least five different concepts of alienation which are used by political scientists, though sociologists make much greater and broader use of the term.

The first type of alienation is referred to as *powerlessness*. This type is often discussed in the positive sense as well, when it is called *efficacy*. Melvin Seeman explains that powerlessness is "the expectancy or probability held by the individual that his own behavior cannot determine ... the outcomes ... he seeks."[8] Powerlessness can have multiple dimensions, just as the concept of alienation does.

In one sense, powerlessness means that the individual believes that he cannot affect government in its decisions because of some fault of the government. He feels that the government is somehow not responsive because of its own faults. The positive side of this concept is called *external efficacy*. Conversely, an individual may believe that he cannot affect government simply because of his own inadequacies. In this instance the government is not perceived as faulty, but rather the individual himself. In a positive sense, this is called *internal efficacy*. In either case the individual will feel separated from the government.

A second frequently discussed form of alienation is sometimes called *anomie*. This particular type of alienation may be defined as *normlessness, distrust,* or *cynicism,* though these three terms are not always used interchangeably. Anomie occurs when an individual feels that the performance of government and its leadership is inappropriate and violates widely accepted norms. A state of anomie occurs when an individual has high expectations for government and leaders performing in an acceptable manner. It is the failure to live up to these high expectations which results in the anomic state.

A third type of political alienation involves *meaninglessness*. When experiencing this condition, the individual believes that there is no discernible pattern to political decision making. It has been observed that "this feeling is illustrated by an individual's inability to distinguish any meaningful political choices, and the sense that political choices are themselves meaningless, because one cannot predict their probable outcomes nor, consequently, use them to change social conditions."[9]

A fourth type of political alienation centers on the notion of *isolation*. This particular type of alienation is activated by an individual's belief that the norms and goals of government and its leaders are "unfair, loaded, illegitimate."[10] This form differs from anomie in that anomie suggests that an individual perceives that others are violating norms which he accepts. But in the case of political isolation, an individual rejects the norms themselves and is not concerned with whether leaders are adhering to them or not.

While the distinctions between the different types of alienation cited above have theoretical importance, it is another thing to find these distinctions made consistently in practical research applications. Survey questions often seem to overlap several different types of alienation or even to constitute an entirely new concept. Therefore, like other researchers, we can be flexible in our use and definition of alienation survey items.

TRENDS IN POLITICAL ALIENATION

The current trend in political alienation began in the mid–1960s. Most nationwide surveys of public opinion have shown that positive evaluations of government and society have declined precipitously since 1964.[11] That the current crisis of confidence began in 1964 is important. Too often journalists and other political observers suggest that public disaffection is a function of Watergate and its related events. But as you can see from the data presented in Table 4–1, Americans had begun to doubt their leaders long before Richard Nixon was elected president in 1968. There can be little doubt that the events of Watergate stimulated and accelerated the trend toward a cynical public, but all of the blame cannot be attributed to Watergate.

The questions presented in Table 4–1 are taken from the SRC-CPS's quadrennial studies of political attitudes. The decline in political trust

Table 4-1
SRC/CPS Measures of Alienation,
Trust and Efficacy, 1964–1980

Trust: How much of the time do you think you can trust the government in Washington to do what is right—just about always, most of the time, or only some of the time?

	1964	1968	1972	1974	1976	1978	1980
Always	14%	8%	7%	3%	3%	3%	2%
Most of the time	62	53	45	33	29	26	23
Only some of the time/None of the time	22	37	45	61	62	67	73
Don't know/Not ascertained	2	2	3	3	1	4	2
	100%	100%	100%	100%	100%	100%	100%

Big interests: Would you say the government is pretty much run by a few big interests looking out for themselves or that it is run for the benefit of all the people?

	1964	1968	1972	1974	1976	1978	1980
For benefit of all.	64%	52%	43%	24%	24%	24%	21%
Few big interests	29	39	48	65	66	65	70
Other/Depends/ Both	4	5	3	3	2	1	–
Don't know/Not ascertained	3	4	6	8	8	10	9
	100%	100%	100%	100%	100%	100%	100%

Honesty: Do you think that quite a few of the people running the government are a little crooked, not very many people are, or hardly any of them are crooked at all?

	1964	1968	1972	1974	1976	1978	1980
Hardly any	18%	18%	16%	10%	13%	12%	9%
Not many	48	49	46	41	40	41	41
Quite a few	29	25	34	45	41	39	46
Don't know/Not ascertained	5	8	4	4	6	8	4
	100%	100%	100%	100%	100%	100%	100%

Efficacy: People like me don't have any say about what the government does.

	1964	1968	1972	1974	1976	1978	1980
Agree	29%	41%	36%	40%	41%	45%	39%
Disagree	69	58	63	57	56	52	59

Table 4-1
SRC/CPS Measures of Alienation,
Trust and Efficacy, 1964-1980
(Continued)

Don't know/Not ascertained.....	2	1	1	3	3	3	2
	100%	100%	100%	100%	100%	100%	100%

Source: SRC/CPS Election Studies.

is best captured in the first SRC/CPS question which asks persons to rate how much of the time they think they can trust the government in Washington to do what is right. As Table 4-1 indicates, in 1964, 76 percent of those surveyed felt that you can trust the government in Washington always or most of the time to do what is right. By 1980, this figure had declined to 26 percent. So in one decade the American public made a substantial reassessment of its orientations toward the trustworthiness of Washington.

But government is not the only institution singled out for public criticism. The second item in Table 4-1 suggests that Americans grew increasingly distrustful of big interests during the years between 1964 and 1980. Only 29 percent felt that government was run by a few big interests in 1964. By 1980 more than twice that number, 70 percent, believed that government was run by a few big interests looking out for themselves. The third question in the table demonstrates tremendous growth of the belief that there are crooks in government. This may stem from concern about the growing power of "special interests."

The last item in Table 4-1 deals with political efficacy, or a person's belief that he or she can influence government. It is clear that there has been an increase in the belief that we cannot have much say about what the government does. But this trend is not as constant, nor has the change been as spectacular as for political trust. As some have noted, the trends in political efficacy and political trust are not necessarily related to each other. Nevertheless, Americans in 1980 were less likely to feel politically efficacious than was the populace in the 1960s.

The trend in alienation and powerlessness is further demonstrated by the data presented in Table 4-2. The survey items included in the table form the basis of a scale of alienation, powerlessness, and cynicism used by the Louis Harris polling firm since 1966. The data show that between 1966 and 1980 there was an increase of 34 percent in the average percentage of respondents reporting feelings of alienation and powerlessness as measured by this scale.

Table 4–2
**Trends in Alienation and Powerlessness Felt by Americans,
1966–1982**

| | Percentage of Respondents Agreeing | | | | | |
Statement	1966	1968	1976	1980	Change 1966– 1980	1982
The rich get richer and the poor get poorer.	45%	54%	78%	78%	+33%	72%
What you think doesn't count much anymore	37	42	63	64	+27	58
People running the country don't really care what happens to you	26	36	64	50	+24	50
Feel left out of things going on around you	9	12	45	48	+39	43
Average feeling alienated and powerless	29%	36%	62%	60%	+34%	56%

Source: Harris Polls.

This average change was influenced most by massive changes in attitudes on two of the items. The second greatest change came on the item which measured the belief that "The rich get richer and the poor get poorer." In 1966 45 percent of the Harris sample held this belief. By 1980, 78 percent agreed with this statement, a change of 33 points between 1966 and 1980. Greater change was noted on the item which asked respondents to agree or disagree with the statement that "you're left out of things going on around you." Only 9 percent of the Harris sample agreed with this statement in 1966, but by 1980 nearly one–half felt that this was true.

On a more positive note, Table 4–2 indicates that Louis Harris's 1982 survey detected a reversal in the alienation trend. On each of the questions asked by Harris, more positive attitudes were expressed in 1982 than at any time since 1974. Only time can tell whether this turnaround in attitudes will continue.

Both the Harris data and SRC/CPS items suggest that political alienation increased after 1964 on almost every dimension which was discussed earlier in this chapter. In the following pages, we will examine questions regarding the objects of this change in political alienation. We will attempt to see whether alienation is directed toward our system of government or more narrowly toward the incumbent officeholders during this era of change. We will also use the Louis Harris data to examine attitudes toward selected institutions, both political and economic.

OBJECTS OF POLITICAL ALIENATION

The decline in political trust has caused a considerable debate among political scientists. This debate involves questions about attitude objects and centers on the nature of contemporary mass disaffection. Briefly stated, one of the two opposing points of view says that recent declines in traditional support indicators, such as those we have just discussed, portend great danger for the American system of government. As David Easton has noted, these political scientists believe the United States "is now suffering a 'crisis of regime.' "[12] Juxtaposed to this view is one which holds that Americans are not so much alienated from the system (or the regime, to use Easton's terminology) as they are from incumbent officeholders.

This debate about the nature of declining affection for things political was best captured in a September 1974 exchange in the pages of the *American Political Science Review* between Arthur H. Miller and Jack Citrin.[13] Miller and Citrin were commenting on decline in political trust from 1964 to 1972 as measured by the SRC/CPS items discussed earlier. Despite use of the same data, Miller and Citrin offer different interpretive approaches. Miller sees declining trust as quite serious and an indication that "the whole system of government is threatened." Miller concludes from his examination of the data that increased "distrust of government was partially related to the changing attitudes on the issues of racial integration and U.S. involvement in the Vietnam War." Miller implies further that public malaise over the failure of leaders in institutions to implement satisfactory policies might be generalized into a broader dissatisfaction with the system in general.[14]

Citrin, to the contrary, believes that mistrust such as that recorded in the SRC/CPS measures is largely opposition to incumbents which would not be readily translated into a more general kind of dissatisfaction with the "system." Citrin considers it extremely important that distrusting respondents are no different in their political behavior than their trusting counterparts. As he states, the politically cynical "were as likely as those expressing trust in government to be eligible for good citizenship awards."[15]

This finding, plus the belief that many respondents give distrustful answers because they are "fashionable" led Citrin to see declining trust as considerably less threatening than Miller does. Citrin agrees that many Americans feel that times are bad, but these individuals are not ready to repudiate the American form of government. To make his point, Citrin used the following analogy:

> ... political systems, like baseball teams, have slumps and winning streaks. Having recently endured a succession of losing seasons, Americans boo the home team when it takes the field. But fans are often fickle; victories quickly elicit cheers. And to most fans what matters is whether the home team wins or loses, not how it plays the game.[16]

According to this analysis a modest "winning streak" and, perhaps some new names in the lineup may be sufficient to raise the level of trust in government.

Since the exchange between Citrin and Miller, there have been several new names in the government lineup including two new presidents, Jimmy Carter and Ronald Reagan. Carter seemed to be especially sensitive to what he called the public malaise, prompting him to work aggressively to restore the American people's sense of trust in their government. Recall that in his 1976 inaugural he specifically promised a government for America that is "as good and as competent as its people." Despite the efforts of Carter and other public officials, the public has not been turned around; low levels of trust persist as compared with the 1960s. But the persistence of political alienation still does not tell us whether Miller's argument for distrust of the system or Citrin's argument for distrust of incumbents is most accurate. Only a succession of the lineup changes prescribed by Citrin and some decisive movement in Americans' attitudes is likely to dramatically increase our understanding of the precise meaning of this trend.

CONFIDENCE IN INSTITUTIONS

One rich source of information about American's attitudes toward political institutions is a series of polls conducted by the Louis Harris polling organization. In 1966 and every year from 1971 to the present,

Harris has asked a national sampling of Americans about the amount of confidence vested in leaders of over a dozen prominent political and social institutions. Results of these surveys are presented in Table 4–3.

The most recent surveys confirm that trust in America's leaders remains very low. But the data suggest that distrust in political leaders may be slowing. In the Harris polls, confidence has been declining more in private sector institutions than in public ones. It is especially interesting to note that trust in the news media, which remained relatively high throughout the Watergate period, has dropped to an all–time low point.

Several political institutions' leaders have shown recent increases in public confidence. The White House and Executive Branch ratings went up in 1981, but this might be explained by a "honeymoon effect," in which the public was giving Reagan a early sign of goodwill. This may well fade, however, as it has for some other presidents. Perhaps more significant are the numbers for Congress. That institution reached its low mark in 1976 when only 9 percent of those interviewed had a great deal of confidence in its leadership. Since that time, Congress has received consistently better evaluations, although they are still well below those given Congress before 1973.

The Harris organization's analyses of these trends warns that "it is important to point out that Americans are giving their reactions to each institution as a whole."[17] When asked to evaluate their own congressman rather than Congress as a whole, or when asked to evaluate their own union leader rather than union leaders generally, people almost always give their own leader a higher rating. Political scientists have similarly observed the tendency of many persons to love their congressman while hating Congress. This phenomenon explains, at least in part, why the downward trend in public confidence has not resulted in more elected officials being driven from office at reelection time.

WHO IS ALIENATED?

Flanigan and Zingale wrote in 1975 that decreasing levels of political trust in "the last decade or so" focused upon three important population subgroups. Those affected were:

Table 4-3
Levels of Confidence in People Running American Institutions, 1966-1981

"As far as the people in charge of running the following institutions are concerned, would you say you have a great deal of confidence, only some confidence, or hardly any confidence at all in them?"

	Percentage expressing "great deal of confidence" in leaders											
	1981	1980	1979	1978	1977	1976	1975	1974	1973	1972	1971	1966
Medicine	37	34	30	42	43	42	43	49	57	48	61	73
Higher educational institutions	34	36	33	41	37	31	36	40	44	33	37	61
The U.S. Supreme Court	29	27	28	29	29	22	28	34	33	28	23	50
The military	28	28	29	29	27	23	24	29	40	35	27	61
The White House	28	18	15	14	31	11	X	18	18	X	X	X
The executive branch of the federal government	24	17	17	14	23	11	13	18	19	27	23	41
Television news	24	29	37	35	28	28	35	32	41	X	X	X
Organized religion	22	22	20	34	29	24	32	32	36	30	27	41
Major companies	16	16	18	22	20	16	19	15	29	27	27	55
Congress	16	18	18	10	17	9	13	16	X	21	19	42
The press	16	19	28	23	18	20	26	25	30	18	18	29
Law firms	16	13	16	18	14	12	16	17	24	X	X	X
Organized labor	12	14	10	15	14	10	14	18	20	15	14	22

Source: Harris Polls   X = not asked

... blacks who became discouraged by the failure of government programs to promote social and economic progress; people, particularly young people, who became frustrated at their failure to reverse the policy of military involvement in Southeast Asia; and a third group of people who became increasingly alarmed over the unwillingness of the government to deal firmly with the other two groups.[18]

Trends in the alienation of each of these groups are considered below.

Black Political Cynicism

Studies of political cynicism or distrust frequently focus on the attitudes of black Americans. Political distrust by blacks is not particularly surprising when one considers that much of the political attitude literature links negativism with social and economic deprivation. What has surprised some observers, though, is that SRC/CPS studies of trust in government show that blacks were more trusting than whites from 1964 to 1968.[19] This tide of black trust undoubtedly sprang from an acknowledgment by blacks that government, at least the federal government, was making serious attempts to improve the economic, social, and political condition of America's black people. Miller has specifically linked black satisfaction to passage of the 1964 Civil Rights Act.[20]

Whatever the cause of black trust in the early to midsixties, the precipitous drop in black political trust to below that of whites in every SRC/CPS survey after 1966 prompts more difficult questions of causality. Miller has hypothesized that advances brought about in the early and midsixties by the civil rights movement created expectations among blacks which could not be fulfilled in the latter part of the sixties. Miller also presents data which suggest that while the Vietnam involvement caused distrust of government among both blacks and whites, it had an earlier and more profound impact on the blacks' attitudes. This could be explained, perhaps, by the fact that the black community was more "personally" involved in the Vietnam War, blacks having served in disproportionate numbers in the armed forces which fought in that war. Miller's thesis, we conclude, is that political cynicism is greater among blacks than whites primarily because of blacks' less favorable evaluations of policies of the federal level of government.[21]

We do not wholeheartedly agree with Miller. After studying SRC/

CPS and Louis Harris data, we feel that analysis of the origins of post-1966 political cynicism should take into account blacks' evaluations of state and local governments as well as their evaluation of the federal government. Our reasoning is based on data presented in Tables 4-4 (Harris data) and 4-5 (SRC/CPS Data) which show that, at least prior to 1976, blacks were less cynical than whites in their attitudes toward the federal government. Furthermore, the data demonstrate that prior to 1976 blacks' confidence in the federal government always exceeded that of whites. Taken together, these findings suggest strongly that early declines in black trust in government were prompted by unfavorable evaluations by blacks of the policies of state and local governments. More recently, however, blacks' confidence in the federal government has fallen to the level of whites while blacks' general political trust lags well behind the whites.

Other data imply that blacks are not ready for a radical restructuring of American government, as black leaders often suggest. Harris 1973 survey data presented in Table 4-6 indicate that few blacks want any level of government to be weakened. Blacks, as compared with whites, want a stronger government at every level. These data suggest that blacks are not experiencing a crisis of diffuse support. Of course, a persistent distrust of leaders by blacks could begin to erode the diffuse support of blacks, but as of this time that process seems to be quite limited. Blacks realize that government is, or has been, solving some of their problems, and they have consequently developed a limited sense of confidence in government.

Age and Political Alienation

The second group of disaffected Americans identified by Flanigan and Zingale were the young and others "who became frustrated at their failure to reverse the police of military involvement in Southeast Asia."[22] The alienation of youth during the Vietnam era was vividly portrayed in every media source. Youthful alienation was new to Americans.

Flanigan and Zingale noted in 1975 that:

> ... over the last fifteen years [before Vietnam, etc.] the youngest voters have typically been the most trusting of government, even as general levels of trust have declined, a tendency one would expect given their recent exposure to the educational process that at least in part sees itself as building support for the system.[23]

Table 4–4
Degrees of Cynicism for Local, State, and Federal Levels of Government, by Race, 1973

Degree of	Percentage of Respondents Expressing Cynicism about Different Levels of Government					
	Local		State		Federal	
Cynicism	White	Black	White	Black	White	Black
Low	68%	59%	69%	62%	32%	42%
Medium..........	25	31	22	31	38	40
High	7	10	9	7	30	18
	100%	100%	100%	100%	100%	100%

Note: White subsample, N = 1,404; black subsample, N = 121. The measure of cynicism was based on two questions: 1) "Compared to five years ago, do you feel you have more confidence, less confidence, or about the same amount of confidence in (local/state/federal) government as you had then?"; and (2) "As far as you personally are concerned, do you feel that (local/state/federal) government has improved the quality of life in the past few years, made it worse, or not changed it much either way?"
Source: Harris Poll data, 1973.

Table 4–5
Expression of Greater Confidence in National Than State or Local Government, by Race

	Percentage of Respondents Expressing More Confidence in National Government	
	White	Black
1968...	43%	59%
1972...	42	51
1974...	29	38
1976...	29	29

Note: Question not asked in surveys after 1976.
Source: SRC/CPS Election Studies.

These authors suggested that the socialization process may not have provided youth of the 1960s and 1970s with a deep enough reservoir of support to mediate their indignation toward the Vietnam conflict and fear of the draft. Flanigan and Zingale also imply that youth were more affected by Vietnam and early Watergate revelations because they had the "least firmly established attitudes" before such events.[24]

Table 4-6

Suggested Changes in Strength of Various Levels of Government, by Race, 1973

Percentage of Respondents Suggesting Changes in Government of Various Levels

Level of government should be:	Local		State		Federal	
	White	Black	White	Black	White	Black
Made much stronger	26%	32%	22%	27%	16%	26%
Only somewhat stronger	35	29	37	33	15	15
Somewhat less strong	5	3	8	5	30	14
Power taken away	3	2	3	4	14	11
Kept as is (voluntary)	24	19	23	14	18	15
Not sure	7	15	7	16	8	19
	100%	100%	100%	99%	101%	100%

Source: U.S. Congress, Senate, Committee on Government Operations, Confidence and Concern: Citizens View American Government, 93rd Cong., 1st Sess., 1973, Part II, pp. 123–24.

But whatever the cause and magnitude of youthful negativism, in the 1960s and 1970s the most severely alienated group of Americans in recent years is persons sixty-five and older. The alienation of the aged has gone largely without notice by the media, probably because the "meager outcries (of the aged) have been constantly upstaged by the dramatic indignation of youth."[25]

Robert Gilmour and Robert Lamb have used SRC/CPS data collected from 1960 to 1972 to analyze age and its relationship to what they call "extreme alienation." This attitude structure is defined as a combination of three distinct feelings: "distrust of government and politicans, a sense of meaninglessness of . . . political choices, and personal powerlessness to influence . . ." American politics. Gilmour and Lamb show that "in 1968 and again in 1972, extreme alienation was the response of nearly 30 percent of Americans over age sixty-five." Youthful alienation was far below this figure in 1968 and 1972. Gilmour and Lamb have concluded from extensive interviewing that "the elderly have been inescapably buffeted by long lifetimes of unprecedented change," and are frequently "cast aside by family and friends to the isolation of institutional 'homes' and retirement communities," caught in the squeeze between stagnant social security benefits and double–digit inflation.[26]

During the 1960s and 1970s, trust was lowest among the youngest and oldest age groups in the electorate. But with the end of the Vietnam War, and the waning resentment over Watergate, young Americans are once again relatively more trusting as they were before these traumatic events. In the meantime, older Americans remain more alienated. Table 4–7 compares the alienation of various age groups in 1980. The measure of alienation is explained later in the chapter in the trend assessment section. While the data presented in the table are similar to data from the 1960s, there is somewhat less difference between the three groups. Older persons are not much more alienated than their younger counterparts. And middle–aged Americans, perhaps influenced by the infusion of alienated youth of the 1960s and 1970s, are not less alienated than the other two groups.

Table 4–7
Political Alienation, by Age, 1980

	Age		
	18–29	*30–49*	*50 & over*
Percentage "alienated"	28	29	32

Source: SRC/CPS Election Studies

The Newly Alienated

Flanigan and Zingale identified the third major group of disaffected Americans as those who became alarmed over the government's response (or lack of response) to civil rights and Vietnam protests. Miller has characterized these Americans as "cynics of the right."[27] Former Vice President Spiro Agnew dubbed these Americans "the silent majority." He and other politicians, like George Wallace, said that this group of disaffected Americans had been silent and ignored far too long in American politics.

Richard Dawson has suggested that skilled laborers like construction workers are typical of the silent majority Agnew sought to represent. Regarding their attitudes, Dawson states that "skilled workers have the highest incidence of negative attitudes." He notes further:

> The skilled worker tends to see the government supporting or engaging in programs and actions designed to aid the very poor. Rightly or wrongly, he often perceives these efforts as operating at his expense rather than for his benefit. He sees the sons and daughters of the privileged engaging in riots, demonstrations, and other behavior generally considered immoral or illegal, for which they receive little or no punishment. He sees the young flouting the values of hard work, patriotism, and respect for law and authority, which he was taught must be abided by and believed in for acceptance and success. He sees a government that seems responsive not to his interests and needs, but instead to those of others, many of whom he sees as less deserving. These are the types of discontent Wallace sought to exploit in the 1968 election and again in the 1972 Democratic primaries.[28]

While Dawson's analysis has focused on skilled workers, there is some speculation that similar discontent has spread to other middle-class, even white–collar, occupational groups. James Q. Wilson, referring to Arthur Miller's analysis of SRC/CPS data, notes that the most extensive decline in public confidence from 1958 to 1972 occurred among those persons earning middle-range incomes. Middle–income blacks and whites lost more ground in confidence than lower–and higher–income persons of either race. Wilson contends that middle–class discontent springs from the "rise of problems deeply affecting the middle class which the government would like to solve but cannot."[29] He cites crime and other issues related to public order as examples of unsolvable problems. Miller similarly states that his "cynics of the right" have a fixation on social control issues.[30]

Table 4-8
Political Alienation for Selected
Socio-Economic Groups, 1980

Group	Percentage "alienated"
Income less than $10,000	42
Income $10,000 to $24,999	32
Income $25,000 and over	23
Blue-collar workers	34
Sales and clerical workers	25
Managerial and administrative workers	28
Professional workers	13
Grade school education	45
High school education	31
Some college education (no degree)	19
College degree	16
Self-described "Average working class"	37
Self-described "Upper working class"	29
Self-described "Average middle class"	24
Self-described "Upper middle class"	21

Source: SRC/CPS Election Study

Data collected in the 1980 SRC/CPS election survey suggest that political alienation among middle-class groups may be on the wane. With the turbulence of the civil rights movement, Vietnam, and Watergate behind the nation, middle-class Americans may be regaining their lost sense of trust in political leaders and institutions. Using the measure of political alienation we will introduce later in the trend assessment section of this chapter, we have compiled data on the level of alienation among several socio-economic groups in Table 4-8. It is clear that by 1980 political alienation was once again concentrated at the lower end of the socio-economic spectrum, among persons making incomes of less than $10,000, blue-collar workers, persons with a grade school education, and those who think of themselves as "average working class." While the data suggest that alienation may linger among some of the newly alienated, such as better-educated and -paid blue collar workers, it is obvious that the staunchly middle class, especially the college educated and professionals, can in no way be characterized as seriously alienated. The middle classes have once again become some of the most trusting citizens, even if they briefly flirted with alienation in the 1970s.

In conclusion, the trend toward increased alienation among several groups during the 1960s and 1970s, most notably the young and the middle classes, seems to have abated. These groups are once again relatively more satisfied with the actions of government. But the trend toward relatively greater alienation among blacks, the poor, and the aged seems to be continuing. And with the economic hard times of the early 1980s, it seems probable that these groups will remain relatively cynical about public affairs. Only a significant turnaround in the economic security of these groups is likely to correct their perception that the political process serves the well-to-do while ignoring the plight of those less fortunate.

ALIENATION AND CONTACT WITH GOVERNMENT

In explaining the origins of political alienation in the United States as people's responses to unpopular policies, our premise has been that alienation from government is a shared response to policies which disadvantage a class of persons. While alienation may be propagated among some Americans in this fashion, for many others the road to alienation may be an individual rather than group experience. Some political journalists and political scientists have suggested that alienation may have its origins in an unsatisfactory personal experience with government officials.

Personal experiences with government and government officials may take several forms. A relatively small segment of the population has engaged in self-initiated contact with government. Surveys conducted on national and local levels have consistently shown that up to 20 percent of Americans have contacted government officials.[31] According to Sidney Verba and Norman Nie, self-initiated contact is the *only* form of political participation engaged in by 4 percent of Americans.[32]

Many more Americans come into contact with government officials without self-initiation of the contact. They may be compelled to appear before government officials for routine matters such as renewal of a driver's license, obtaining a permit to fish in public waters, or registering to vote. In such matters an individual problem or complaint is seldom involved, the contact is engaged in by most Americans, and is usually initiated by a government agency rather than by the individual.

Whether contact is initiated by government or coincidental, research by Herbert Jacob and by Robert Weissberg, and by a Survey Research Center team directed by Daniel Katz, has indicated that unsatisfactory experiences with government officials are not generalized into more comprehensive forms of alienation.[33]

A different set of findings characterizes the relationship between self-initiated contact and generalized alienation. Tim Ryles finds citizens who have contacted a government official and judged that contact to be unsuccessful are likely to experience lower levels of political trust and efficacy. Similar findings were made in a 1973 Harris study. Among persons who reported initiating contact with government, those who were dissatisfied with their experience were more likely than satisfied respondents to be generally cynical about the level of government with which they had experienced a problem. These data, shown in Table 4-9, indicate that persons reporting an unsatisfactory experience with state government are three times as likely to hold a highly cynical view of state government as those who said they were satisfied with their contact.

The Harris data show that few Americans initiate contact with government and, further, that many Americans are satisfied with such contacts. This could lead us to conclude that bureaucratic encounters have been only a minor stimulus to the trend toward widespread political alienation. But, as Louis Harris stated before Congress, only one in twenty Americans has had a *highly* satisfying encounter with an official of our national government.[34] Thus there is reason to study citizen–government interaction carefully if alienation continues to increase.

A TREND ASSESSMENT: ALIENATION

The concept of trust or alienation discussed in this chapter is subject to disagreement among scholars. There is agreement, however, that it is of little constructive benefit to a society for its citizens to distrust its officials. It may be that the growing distrust evident, especially since the early 1960s, is an innocuous and isolated belief which is increasingly held by the general public but is unrelated to any disruptive or threatening political action or inaction by citizens. At best, however, no social benefit can be found in this increasing public alienation.

In our assessment of this trend we will examine the political behavior

Table 4-9

Degree of Cynicism Toward Government Related to Satisfaction with Self-Initiated Contact, by Level of Government (Numbers in Parentheses)

LOCAL GOVERNMENT

Degree of Cynicism	Have Not Contacted	Have Contacted		
		Whole Subsample	Those Highly Satisfied	Those Not Satisfied at All
Low	67%	66%	76%	46%
Medium	26	27	21	40
High	7	7	3	14
Total	100%	100%	100%	100%
	(1,182)	(393)	(154)	(134)

STATE GOVERNMENT

Degree of Cynicism	Have Not Contacted	Have Contacted		
		Whole Subsample	Those Highly Satisfied	Those Not Satisfied at All
Low	68%	68%	80%	51%
Medium	23	22	15	34
High	9	10	5	15
Total	100%	100%	100%	100%
	(1,354)	(219)	(81)	(74)

Table 4-9
Degree of Cynicism Toward Government Related to Satisfaction with Self-Initiated Contact, by Level of Government (Numbers in Parentheses) (Continued)

Degree of Cynicism	FEDERAL GOVERNMENT Have Not Contacted	Whole Subsample	Have Contacted Those Highly Satisfied	Those Not Satisfied at All
Low	34%	30%	38%	14%
Medium	38	34	27	33
High	28	36	35	53
Total	100%	100%	100%	100%
	(1,403)	(182)	(78)	(43)

Note: Wordings of questions used to construct cynicism measures are reported in the note to Table 4–4.
Source: Harris Poll data, 1973.

of those who find their public officials unresponsive. We might expect, for example, that those who are distrustful or alienated are less inclined to vote. Thus, the decline in turnout might be explained by the increase of alienation within the public. Defection and independence from political parties might well be the result of the alienation felt by issue-oriented voters who see little choice among the candidates nominated by the major political parties. For the first time, then, we can combine assessments of all the trends discussed in this book.

Are declining public participation, a growth in independency, and more frequent deviating elections the result of an issue-responsive public which is growing increasingly distrustful of its public officials? Or are these trends unrelated to one another? To answer this we offer an assessment of the relationship between alienation and the previously developed measure of defections, independency, participation, and quality of candidate evaluation.

While SRC/CPS surveys conducted since 1952 have included many questions which pertain to the confidence people express in government and public officials, our assessment over time of political alienation is restricted by the limited number of questions which have been included in every survey. We have chosen to focus on two questions asked in each survey since 1952 that seem germane to alienation from political officials. The questions are:

> I don't think public officials care much what people like me think.
>   Agree_____ Disagree_____
> People like me don't have any say about what government does.
>   Agree_____ Disagree_____

We classified respondents who agreed with both questions as *alienated*. All other responses were classified as *less alienated* or *trusting*. Of the sample in 1952, twenty percent were alienated. This remained relatively stable in 1956, 16%; 1960, 16%; and 1964, 21%. In 1968 alienation rose to 35%. This level remained in 1972, 31% and 1976, 36% but fell sharply in 1980 to 26%. This apparent decline in political alienation in 1980 greatly complicates our reaching a conclusion. It may mean that alienation has peaked as is suggested by some recent Harris surveys we discussed. Or it may be that 1980 was an abnormal election year and that 1984 will see alienation climb above the 30 percent level again.

The growth of issue-oriented evaluation of the presidential candidates appears unrelated to changing levels of alienation in the country.

Figure 4–1
Relationship Between Presidential
Candidate Evaluation and Alienation

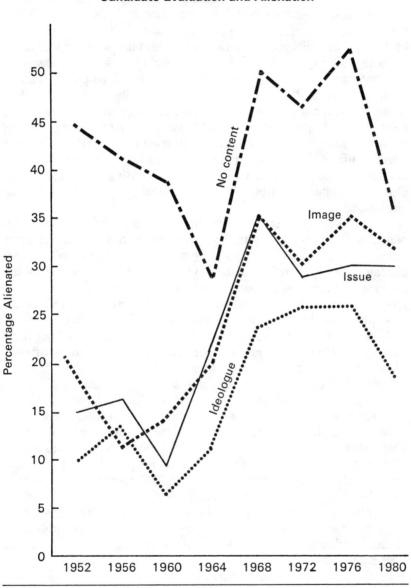

Source: SRC/CPS Election Studies.

Figure 4–1 shows that both the best (issue and ideologue) and the worst (image and no–content) of the evaluations of the candidates have been similarly affected by changing patterns of political alienation since 1960. Ideological, issue–oriented, and image evaluators have differed little in the extent of their alienation. But those respondents who were unable to describe any difference between the candidates which would cause them to vote for one rather than the other, those we have classed as no–content evaluators, have proven consistently to be the most alienated. Even in the 1950s they already exceeded the alienation evident in the 1970s among those more capable of evaluating the candidates. Issue–oriented candidate evaluators have not been exceptional in their contribution to the alienation of the American electorate. Rather it is those unaffected by the increasing sophistication of the electorate that continue to be alienated. In short, the increasing alienation of the electorate cannot be attributed to the increasing issue orientation of the electorate.

The relationship between alienation and party identification depicted in Figure 4–2 varies greatly between elections. At various times independents, Republicans, and Democrats have each been the most alienated, but all three seem to have been similarly affected by the increase of alienation affecting the country at large. In 1976 and 1980 independents were more alienated than Democrats and Democrats more alienated than Republicans, a pattern that is not unlike that noted in 1952 at a somewhat lower overall level of alienation. Given these trends, we cannot conclude that the growth in independency results from increases in political alienation.

Defection from one's political party is related to political alienation as shown in Figure 4–3. In 1968 and in 1980, little difference in alienation was notable between those who defected in at least one vote for president, senator, or representative and those who were loyal in their votes. But between 1968 and 1976, defectors were somewhat more alienated. However, this difference should not be exaggerated, as it is only 7 percent in 1976 (30 percent versus 37 percent highly alienated). But taken in conjunction with the lack of difference noted among independents, this difference suggests that some citizens perceive the opposition party as an alternative leadership to which they can turn. It is not necessary, therefore, to abandon political parties for their failure to offer a choice.

Participation shows no consistent relationship to alienation over time. Until 1968, quite contrary to expectations, the alienated were

Figure 4-2
Relationship Between Political Party
Identification and Alienation

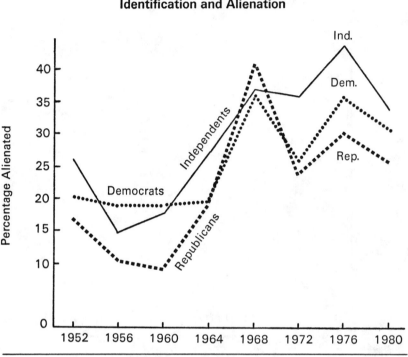

Source: SRC/CPS Election Studies.

increasingly likely to participate, at least to the extent of voting in presidential elections. The figures are: in 1952, 58 percent of the alienated voted; 1956, 58 percent; 1960, 64 percent; 1964, 73 percent; 1968, 71 percent; 1972, 58 percent; 1976, 57 percent; and 1980, 58 percent. Thus better than half of those with little trust in the public officials nevertheless vote for president. This, of course, is substantially short of the 75 percent turnout typically achieved by the less alienated.

These data mean that the alienated do vote less than more trusting people do. But as alienation increased, the alienated actually voted

Figure 4–3
Relationship Between Defection From
Political Party and Alienation

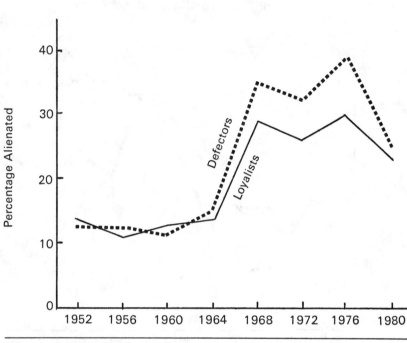

Source: SRC/CPS Election Studies.

more, becoming a larger group within the voting part of the electorate (in the 1950s about 1 voter in 6 was alienated, while in 1980 better than 1 in 4 were alienated). Both the likelihood of the alienated to vote and their share of all voters peaked in 1968. These findings do not form the foundations for any definitive conclusions about alienation and voting. Nevertheless, we believe it is most important to remember that a majority of the alienated continue to express some hope for and faith in our system of government by turning out to vote in presidential elections.

Conclusions

Not unlike the other variables we have considered in the two preceding chapters, political alienation does not appear to play a central role in unraveling the mysteries of American electoral behavior. It explains neither why people are less likely to vote today than two decades ago nor what factors are more likely to influence the candidate choice of those who do vote. The decline of political alienation in 1980 reinforces our conclusion that this phenomenon is not responsible for some of the other trends we have observed. In the face of declining alienation, defections from political party soared, participation continued to decline (although not sharply so), and the quality of candidate evaluation improved. Were alienation central to accounting for the other trends in electoral behavior, we would have expected the opposite result in terms of the defection rate, turnout, and candidate evaluation. Indeed, in looking closely at the relationships between alienation and our other trends, we find a weakened relationship in 1980 in almost every instance.

Taken together, our findings about change in political trust and alienation do not absolutely refute the notion that contemporary disaffection might render serious damage to our republic. We generally agree with theorists who stress the philosophy that a government needs the support of its citizenry in order to function satisfactorily. But, as we have demonstrated in this chapter, the fact that many Americans are reluctant to give their unqualified support to the government does not signal the undoing of our party and electoral systems. Therefore, while we urge continued research into the causes and effects of alienation among the masses, we do not believe that alienation currently represents a force which threatens the stability of the American electorate or system of government.

NOTES

1. David Easton and Jack Dennis found that children believe the president is more persistent, diligent, and likely to keep promises than their own fathers. *Children in the Political System* (New York: McGraw-Hill, 1969), pp. 249–72.

2. David Easton, *A Systems Analysis of Political Life* (New York: John Wiley & Sons, 1965).

3. The definitions of type of political support cited here are from David Easton's latest restatement of his concepts: "A Re-Assessment of the Concept of Political Support," *British Journal of Political Science* 5 (October 1975): 435–57.

4. Easton, *Systems Analysis of Political Life*, p. 220.

5. William H. Flanigan and Nancy H. Zingale, *Political Behavior of the American Electorate* (Boston: Allyn and Bacon, 1975), p. 183.

6. Edward N. Muller, "A Test of a Partial Theory of Potential for Political Violence," *American Political Science Review* 66 (September 1972): 954.

7. Arthur H. Miller, "Political Issues and Trust in Government: 1964–1970," *American Political Science Review* 68 (September 1974): 951.

8. Melvin Seeman, "On the Meaning of Alienation," *American Sociological Review* 24 (December 1959): 783–91.

9. Ada Finifter, "Dimensions of Political Alienation," *American Political Science Review* 64 (June 1970): 390.

10. Ibid., p. 391.

11. Miller, "Political Issues and Trust in Government."

12. Easton, "Re-Assessment of Concept of Political Support," p. 435.

13. Miller, "Political Issues and Trust in Government"; Jack Citrin, "Comment: The Political Relevance of Trust in Government," *American Political Science Review* 68 (September 1974): 973–88; Arthur H. Miller, "Rejoinder to 'Comment' by Jack Citrin: Political Discontent or Ritualism?" *American Political Science Review* 68 (September 1974): 989–1001.

14. Miller, "A Rejoinder to 'Comment' by Jack Citrin."

15. Citrin, "Comment," p. 984.

16. Ibid., p. 987.

17. Press release issued by The Harris Survey, October 22, 1981.

18. Flanigan and Zingale, *Political Behavior of American Electorate*, p. 183.

19. Miller, "Political Issues and Trust in Government," p. 955.

20. Ibid.

21. Miller, "Rejoinder to 'Comment' by Jack Citrin," p. 990, states that on a "practical, operational level, political trust may be treated as an affective orientation toward the 'government in Washington'—the most salient level of government in the United States."

22. Flanigan and Zingale, *Political Behavior of American Electorate*, p. 183.

23. Ibid., pp. 181–82.

24. Ibid., p. 182.

25. Robert S. Gilmour and Robert B. Lamb, *Political Alienation in Contemporary America* (New York: St. Martin's Press, 1975), p. 63.

26. Ibid., p. 67.

27. Miller, "Political Issues and Trust in Government," p. 962.

28. Richard E. Dawson, *"Public Opinion and Contemporary Disarray* (New York: Harper & Row, 1973), p. 102.

29. James Q. Wilson, "The Riddle of the Middle Class," *The Public Interest* 39 (Spring 1975): 125–29.

30. Miller, "Political Issues and Trust in Government," p. 962.

31. Sidney Verba and Norman H. Nie, *Participation in America* (New York: Harper & Row, 1972), p. 31; Tim Ryles, "The Processing of Citizen Complaints in Local Government" (Paper presented at the Southern Political Science Association meeting, Atlanta 1974; Peter K. Eisinger, "The Pattern of Citizen Contacts with Public Officials," in *People and Politics in Urban Society,* ed. Harlan Hahn (Beverly Hills: Sage Publications, 1971), pp. 43–69.

32. Verba and Nie, *Participation in America,* p. 80.

33. Herbert Jacob, "Contact with Government Agencies: A Preliminary Analysis of the Distribution of Government Services," *Midwest Journal of Political Science* 16 (1972): 123–46; Robert Weissberg, "Adolescent Experiences with Political Authorities," *Journal of Politics* 34 (1972): 797–824; Daniel Katz, Barbara A. Gutek, Robert L. Kahn and Eugenia Barton, *Bureaucratic Encounters* (Ann Arbor, Mich.: Institute for Social Research. 1975).

34. U.S. Congress, Senate, Committee on Government Operations, Subcommittee on Intergovernmental Relations, *Confidence and Concern: Citizens View American Government,* Committee Print, 93rd Congress, 1st Sess, 1973, Part I, p. 115.

CHAPTER 5

The Meaning of Change in American Electoral Behavior

THE PATTERN OF CHANGE IN THE ELECTORATE

As we reflect on trends in American electoral behavior, it is clear that the electorate of the 1980s is different from the one studied by the pioneering political scientists in the 1950s. There are fewer partisans now than then. Issues play a more important role in voters' evaluations of candidates. Americans are increasingly inclined to avoid the polls on election days and a sense of distrust pervades many people's thinking about public affairs and leaders. But despite the obvious fact that the electorate has changed in some regards, we have cautioned throughout this book that the magnitude of change in these trends should not be exaggerated. We are a different electorate today, but not greatly different in most respects.

Despite the absence of sweeping change in American electoral behavior, some political scientists persist in their concern about many of the trends we have examined in this book. As we have noted, the persistence of this professional concern stems from a belief that certain trends may be the harbinger of an era of social and political upheaval. A rather substantial body of political theory supports this concern by arguing, for example, that a government cannot remain stable without the trust and confidence of its citizens. Furthermore, professional concerns about the patterns of change in American electoral behavior point to possible interrelationships between several trends, interrelationships that might accelerate or render irreversible the most feared trends. In this book we

have examined interrelationships among five of these trends in an effort
to determine whether they individually or collectively merit our continued concern. The trends which we have analyzed are:

1. Declining partisanship
2. Increased defection from party voting
3. Increased issue voting
4. Declining voter turnout
5. Declining political trust

Our reasons for examining relationships among these trends are several. If declining turnout, increased defection, increased independency
and declining trust are the common result of a frustrated electorate
which is not satisfied with the alternatives afforded by the major political parties, we cannot be optimistic about America's future. Some
voters may become receptive to demagogues who offer quick solutions
to our nation's problems. Others could come to violate the laws and
norms of our society as their disenchantment grows.

If there is an ever–increasing number of Americans who are impa-
tient with government's failure to adopt certain solutions to the problems faced by our society, and if this impatience makes them less
disposed to accept government policy decisions, government may be
burdened with higher costs to gain public compliance. Furthermore,
these citizens may become receptive to substantial changes in the political process which could disrupt the stability it has enjoyed in our
country for nearly 200 years. Such voters, for example, may press to
make political parties illegal or sharply circumscribe what government
can do by supporting legislation like California's tax–cutting Proposition 13.

This book has sought to determine whether there is evidence of a
substantial group of issue–oriented, less partisan, distrusting citizens
who refuse to participate in the existing political process. Our analysis
has turned on an assessment of the five changes in the electorate named
above and their possible interrelation. We have done this using what
we think are the best measures available, a group of SRC/CPS survey
questions asked in conjunction with each presidential election since
1952. We think each group of questions straightforwardly and validly
assesses relevant attributes of the electorate.

The importance of using identical measures to assess trends and
change cannot be overstated. As some of the studies cited herein have

demonstrated, different data can result in different conclusions. Had we used different questions in different years, the wording of the questions, instead of actual changes, might have been noted. Certainly, even minor changes in the wording of survey questions can alter the response patterns of respondents.

We have measured partisanship and independence from political parties with survey questions in which respondents were asked to express their willingness to identify with a political party or even to admit leaning toward one. Defection was measured by simply comparing survey respondents' votes with their political party identification; defectors do not vote for the candidate of their party. Issue voting was appraised by survey respondents' statements about what would cause them to vote for or against the major political parties' presidential candidates. We have demonstrated that the candidate evaluations of some voters reflect more concern with issues and ideology, causing us to label these people as ideologues or issue oriented. Other voters' judgments are less sophisticated. We have called these voters group–benefit, partisan, image or no–content evaluators based on their particular responses to the candidates. Election turnout has been measured by self–reports of respondents. And finally, political trust has been measured by two survey questions which assess beliefs about one's influence on government and perceptions of the responsiveness of public officials.

These measures confirm many of the trends, although there have been some discontinuities and even reversals in certain trends. Independents have become more numerous (and partisans less numerous), comprising 12 percent of the electorate in 1980 versus 5 percent in 1952. Alienation has also increased, with 36 percent of the SRC/CPS sample being classified as alienated in 1976 versus 20 percent in 1952. This trend may have been reversed in 1980, however, when only 26 percent of those interviewed could be classified as alienated. The quality of candidate evaluations has changed, too. Low quality evaluations based solely on candidate image have declined from 62 percent in 1952 to 22 percent in 1980. Issue–oriented evaluations and defection have fluctuated over the last eight elections. Voting turnout has dropped in a steady fashion since 1960, but we observed that current turnout levels are not much worse than those which occured in the 1940s and 1950s.

Our analysis of the interrelationships among the five trend variables considered yields little support for concern that they are related and comprise a potential danger for our society. The quality of a respondent's candidate evaluation does relate to participation and to alienation, but not in a way consistent with what we might expect. Instead of the issue–oriented evaluators being less participant and more alienated, it is the no–content evaluators that prove distinctive. Typically, only about half of those who say nothing in evaluating presidential candidates vote in presidential contests. No–content evaluators also have been consistently the more alienated citizens.

The quality of the electorate's evaluation of presidential candidates is often thought to be at the root of explanations of how the trends in participation, partisan voting, and alienation are related. This explanation does not appear to be adequate, because while improvements in candidate evaluations can be noted, relationships with participation, partisan voting, and alienation are weak or nonexistent. The pattern of relationships we have found is compatible with the depiction in *The American Voter* of those who are marginally involved in politics as being uninformed, nonparticipant, and least likely to strongly identify with a political party or to vote consistently with party identification.

While independents did not prove to be distinctive in terms of the candidate evaluations, they are somewhat more numerous in contemporary society, and they are voting less. In 1952 only 6 percent of all nonvoters were independents, but in 1980 they comprised 21 percent. But independents prove to be no more alienated than either strong or weak partisans. Issues are no more pivotal to the candidate assessments of independents than they are to those of partisans, and the declining participation of independents is unrelated to their greater alienation. So neither issue orienation nor alienation accounts for the declining participation of independents.

By defining the alienated as those respondents who feel that "officials do not care what people like me think," and that they personally have "no say in what government does," we found some ties with other political behavior but no consistent pattern. Based on 1980 data which compare alienated and more trusting Americans, the alienated are less likely to vote for president, and they are slightly more likely to defect from the political party with which they identify to vote for the opposition party's candidate. But as we have already discussed, alienation is not related to issue or ideological evaluation of a candidate or to independency.

Thus we end up with three clusters of atypical types of citizens: (1) those who have nothing to say when evaluating the candidates, who consistently fail to participate, and who are alienated: (2) the increasingly nonparticipant independents, and (3) the alienated who are consistently less participant and more likely to defect. But each of these groups is a minority when contrasted with the largest group of citizens: the trusting, partisan voters.

OTHER CHANGES IN THE ELECTORATE

Two other changes can be noted in the American electorate since the 1950s, in addition to the trends discussed above. Both of these changes involve significant demographic changes in the electorate. First, Americans are increasingly better educated. Census Bureau figures indicate that the median school years completed for the adult population (twenty-five years of age and older) increased from 10.6 years in 1960 to 12.5 in 1980. There has been an even greater increase in the percentage of the population attending college. In 1960, only 16 percent of the adult population had completed one year or more of college. By 1980, nearly 32 percent had completed one or more year of college and 17 percent had completed four or more years. Thus, the exposure of the electorate to college has more than doubled in just two decades.

Second, changes in the birth rate since 1940 have had and will continue to have an impact on the age distribution of the electorate. The first major change in the birth rate occurred after World War II when veterans in particular married in extraordinary numbers and produced a baby boom. Great numbers of these post–World War II babies became eighteen during the 1970s. Their entrance to the electorate was speeded by the Twenty-sixth Amendment to the U.S. Constitution, enacted in 1971, which lowered the minimum voting age from twenty-one to eighteen years of age. The net result of these events was a lowering of the median age of the electorate. The baby boom cohort will continue to influence the age distribution of the electorate by increasing the median age as its members pass into their middle and elderly years. This is because the birth rate has dropped in almost every year since 1960, meaning that new voters will comprise a smaller and smaller percentage of the electorate for several years to come while the baby boom generation will comprise a larger and larger percentage.

Why are these demographic trends—increased education and a fluctuating birth rate—so important? They are important because education and age are possibly related to some of the other major trends we have discussed. What is confusing, however, is that some political attitudes and behaviors have not gone in the direction that we would expect given the simultaneous changes in demographics. Changes in voter turnout illustrate this puzzle. As we have observed, turnout has declined steadily since the mid–1960s. The change in turnout is perfectly consistent with the change in the age distribution of the electorate. Young voters vote less frequently than their elders, and given that young voters have made up an increasingly greater percentage of the voting age population since 1960, we would expect turnout to decline. Educated voters, however, are more likely to vote than the less educated; and as we have more educated voters now, turnout should have increased. But it has not, constituting a rather intriguing puzzle.

In order to assess the relationship between these two demographic trends and the other trends analyzed in this book, we have divided age and education into three and four categories, respectively. The analysis of age divides the population into three groups: those eighteen to twenty-nine years of age in 1980; those thirty to forty-nine; and those fifty and over. The analysis of education divides persons into four categories: less than high school education; high school; some college; and college degree or more.

Our analysis of data collected in 1980 confirms much that we have learned in previous elections about the relationships between the demographic variables and electoral behavior. In 1980, those between eighteen and twenty-nine years of age constituted only 27 percent of society but represented 39 percent of all independents and 36 percent of nonvoters. The relationship is strongest between age and nonvoting as a majority (53 percent) of respondents between eighteen and twenty-nine did not vote in 1980. Independence from political parties was more common among those in the youngest age category. Twenty percent of those below thirty called themselves independent in 1980 versus 13 percent for those between thirty and forty-nine and 9 percent for those fifty and older. When one combines the impact of youth and independency, the effect on nonvoting is heightened. Only 27 percent of the young (eighteen to twenty–nine year olds) independents bothered to vote in 1980.

The young do not differ in independency and participation alone. Nearly 57 percent of the youngest category of the electorate evaluates candidates in terms of issues rather than images, partisanship, or some other factor. By comparison, 49 percent of those ages thirty to forty-nine and 42 percent of those fifty and over could be classified as issue oriented. But while it may appear that the young clearly are much more sophisticated in their evaluation of candidates, it should also be noted that 15 percent of the young have nothing of substance to say about the presidential candidates. Only about 11 percent of those in the older age categories could be similarly categorized as no content evaluators. In conclusion, however, it seems fair to say that the youngest age group is in sort of a "prepolitics" phase of their political development in which they are capable of issue–based evaluation of candidates, but are not willing to get involved in political activity. Finally, we should note that our analysis failed to reveal any significant relationships between the age groups and our measure of political alienation.

Our analysis of the relationship between education and electoral behavior suggests that all but one of the trends we have discussed have been affected by the increased education of the electorate. The lone exception is the trend in partisan defection. We find that in 1980 the educated tended to be slightly more partisan, equally likely to defect, more participant, less alienated, and more likely to use issues and ideology in evaluating candidates. Persons in the college–educated sector of society are less likely to call themselves independents (12 percent among the college educated versus 14 percent among others). Thus without increasing education, independents would be slightly more common. The impact of education on partisan defection at the ballot box reveals that there is very little difference in defection rates among the various education categories. Differences were apparent for political alienation, however, as only 16 percent of the college educated were alienated in 1980 as compared with 32 percent of the others. It seems that political alienation would be more common if the public were not more educated. The college educated are also more likely to vote; 86 percent of the college educated voted in 1980, compared with 56 percent of those with less education. Thus the decline in turnout has been retarded by education. Finally, education has affected candidate evaluations. In their evaluations of Carter and Reagan (see Table 5-1), the college educated were clearly more likely to use ideology and issues. The less educated were much more likely to articulate evaluations of the candidates which were lower in quality. Nearly half of the less–than–high school education category used image or no–content evaluations of Carter and Reagan. Thus the increase in issue-oriented evaluations noted in an earlier chapter can be explained by the improving education of the American electorate.

In conclusion, we can say, that education has inhibited certain politi-

Table 5-1
Quality of Candidate Evaluations, by Education

Education	Percentage of Respondents Citing Various Types of Candidate Evaluations					
	Ideologue	Issue Oriented	Group Benefit	Partisan	Image	No Content
Less than high school	3%	39%	6%	6%	27%	19%
High school	8	49	3	3	25	12
Some college	15	53	2	6	16	8
College degree or better	20	54	1	6	13	6
N = 1610						

Source: SRC/CPS Election Study, 1980.

cally relevant changes in American society. Were American society to be no better educated today than was the case in the 1950s, participation and partisanship would probably be lower, and alienation and image-oriented evaluations of political candidates would be more common.

CONCLUSIONS

At this point you may wonder whether any substantial conclusions can be noted about the changes in the American electorate. We believe that five conclusions are justified. The first conclusion is that, overall, stability rather than change best characterizes the American electorate over the period 1952-1982. While the American electorate is changing, for example becoming more alienated, this evolution is quite gradual at best and erratic and patternless at worst. In many ways the 1976 election was much closer to that in 1956 than to any election in the interim. If one were forced to pick between the polar adjectives, *changed* and *unchanged,* the electorate seems unchanged.

Second, party identification remains highly predictive as to how people will vote. While the number of independents has more than doubled since 1952, 83 percent of the electorate still identifies with a political party, and 82 percent of these voted for their party's nominee rather than defecting. Thus, at least 72 percent of all votes for major party candidates for president in 1980 are explainable by partisanship in the electorate.

Third, there remains even today a very substantial minority of persons so peripherally involved in politics that even the noisy politics of the presidential campaign gives them nothing to say about the candidates. Such persons also typically fail to vote. It is far more common today, as it was in the 1950s, for nonvoters to be passive bystanders of the political scene rather than zealous proponents or opponents of policy who failed to find a choice among the presidential candidates. Nonparticipant bystanders, rather than nonparticipant zealots, while equally unfortunate for a goal of participant democracy, are probably less threatening to the smooth performance of democracy.

Fourth, verbal assurances of trust for the political system and officials within it, which were common in the 1950s, do not appear as essential as suggested by David Easton and others. We have seen great distrust in the 1970s among voters and nonvoters, among defectors and partisan loyalists, among issue evaluators and those unable to mention any candidate attribute, and among independents and strong partisans. Distrust is common among nearly every type of citizen, meaning that distrust is not at the root of any behaviors we have studied.

Fifth and finally, the forces affecting the electorate over time are not as simple as some theories would suggest. It is not sufficient to tie trends together, based on perceptions of an increasingly issue–oriented electorate which sees little choice among the major political parties and therefore is rebelling into independency, nonvoting, and alienation. No doubt there are Americans who do follow this dynamic pattern, but our analysis suggests this simple theory does not account for the patterns of stability and change which are most notable within the electorate.

Despite these solid conclusions, there have been limits to our analyses. In our assessment of trends in the American electorate, we have used data from large national samples. This has necessarily meant that we are assessing the impact of national trends rather than more limited regional patterns of change. We have also limited our primary analysis to patterns of presidential voting. There is no systematic assessment of congressional or statewide elected office voting comparable to the presidential election studies. There are findings, which must still be judged as tentative, that suggest that congressional and other state- and local-level voting differs somewhat from the patterns found here. It is beyond the scope of our effort to deal with these differences. The reader should be aware, however, that media coverage, public familiarity with the candidates, and participation are all lower in such subpresidential elections. In most respects, presidential voting affords the electorate the greatest opportunity for obtaining information on the candidates and issues associated with an election. This greater, more dynamic, flow of information in presidential campaigns would seem to foretell greater change in future presidential elections than subnational contests.

Similarly, the reader should note that our assessment is limited to but eight presidential elections. We cannot say with confidence which of these few elections were the result of long–term changes in the behavior of the electorate and which were the one–of–a–kind results of unique combinations of presidential candidates. If we had data on many more presidential elections, we might be able to say something definitive about what happens when the Democrats chose a Southerner and the Republicans a Midwesterner, or when the Democrats pick a liberal candidate rather than a moderate, or when the Republicans pick a conservative. Many of our figures show erratic changes over the eight elections. Were we to have many more elections, we might be better able to see underlying long–term changes which transcend these erratic short–term changes. In many ways our speculation, indeed anyone's speculation, about changes in the American electorate is like predicting whether a baseball team will have a good season after having watched its first game or even its first eight games.

The presidential election of 1980 serves as a good example of the dangers associated with trying to use one election's results to predict future trends. Of course, once again in 1980 the minority party won the presidential election as happened previously in 1952, 1956, 1968, and 1972; indeed, Reagan won handily. Many political observers interpreted Reagan's victory, given his ideology, as a conservative mandate for change from the voters. Voters were demanding a break with the past it was claimed. The simultaneous defeats of several liberal U.S. senators seemed to confirm this conclusion. But was this analysis correct? Did the electorate change its course? Did voters respond to the choice of a new solution to our national problems? There are many problems with such an interpretation, especially when viewed from the perspective of the trends we have examined.

While fewer Americans were highly alienated in 1980 than in 1976, participation continued to decline and the alienated continued not to vote. Also, while the number of ideologues did increase, only about one voter in eight was classified as an ideologue in our analysis. Finally, while defection from party did increase, no change in party identification became evident (note the resurgence of Democrats in the 1982 congressional elections); in fact, had John Anderson not been running, defection in 1980 would have been only 18 percent, a figure very close to the normal defection rate across the prior twenty-four years. Therefore, it is possible that the presidential election of 1980 tells us only what happens when a Democratic incumbent president facing calamity in international affairs (e.g., the Iran hostage crisis) and economic problems faces opposition from an attractive Republican candidate and a third party challenger. This interpretation seems more plausible than the "mandate" conclusions discussed above.

WHAT DOES THE FUTURE HOLD?

Throughout this book we have refrained from personal conjecture about the future behavior of the electorate. Instead, we have sought only to summarize what is known about the electoral behavior of Americans. Political science, depending as it does on survey research and actual election results, is not well suited to predicting events that might occur five, ten, or more years from now, but by combining some imagination and logic with a little knowledge, we have developed some ideas about the future directions of each of the trends we have discussed in this book.

Some of our predictions will focus on elections in the next decade or so. Others will focus on events that should not fully unfold for thirty years or more. Some predictions are hopeful in nature while others are dismal. We are more confident in some of the predictions than in others. Our greatest confidence can be vested in predictions which are based on demographic trends which we know will occur (such as the aging of the large baby boom cohort of the electorate) and which involve long–standing relationships (such as the persistent high levels of turnout among middle–aged persons). But all of the predictions which follow are fallible and subject to revision and change as the future unfolds.

Political Partisanship in the Future

Two probable nonelectoral trends of the future seem likely to have an impact on partisanship and other political trends. First, the post-

World War II baby boom cohort will be the dominant population group in America for many years to come. They will reach their fifties in about two decades and enter retirement in three. Assuming normal mortality rates for this group, we can expect it to be the largest chunk of the population for another forty years at least. Second, it seems certain that government as well as other institutions will be faced with increasingly technical and complicated decisions in the future. Two factors seem to insure this outcome: the increased use of computers and other sophisticated analytical devices allow mankind to make policies in areas heretofore inaccessible to decision makers; and, technological innovation frequently has by-products which may adversely affect society, the environment, and the individual. Examples of issues enmeshed with such technical considerations are easy to imagine. What mix of weapon systems should the U.S. military employ to the year 2000 to counterbalance the Soviet threat? What accounting conventions should be used in calculating the rate base for public gas and electric utilities? What should be the maximum allowable amount of a trace toxic metal in public drinking water supplies? The list of probable questions is practically endless.

We expect that the baby boom cohort and the importance of technical matters will both impinge on political partisanship, but perhaps with very different effects. Because we know that attachment to political parties increases as persons become older, as the baby boom cohort ages, its large size in the electorate should result in a more partisan electorate. Only two things seem likely to counteract this. There could be a new baby boom which would add millions of new voters without strong partisanship into the electorate about the time the baby boom cohort reaches its fifties and sixties. Or the baby boom cohort could defy conventional wisdom and remain aloof from the political parties in their middle and elderly years. The latter seems to be a distinct possibility because the baby boom cohort has always been somewhat different. It came into the electorate less partisan and less participant than most other cohorts before or since. Some political scientists have speculated that this stems from the turbulence of the period when the baby boom cohort came of age politically. That period included the last days of the civil rights movement, the horror of Vietnam, and the drama of Watergate. Exposure to these events may have had a lasting effect on the political behavior of this cohort.

We expect that technological developments may loosen the bonds of partisanship or at least may weaken parties as influential participants in political decision making. We base this prediction on the belief that technological matters will require governments to rely more and more on technical experts for guidance and direction, and less on political parties and other traditional participants in the policy–making process. Political parties are not likely to offer the sophisticated structuring of opinion necessary to guide decisions on such technical issues. The net result may be that the electorate comes to see political parties, and perhaps attachments to party, as an anachronism. Scientists, engineers, and other experts may become the opinion leaders rather than political figures.

Other factors also point toward the possible further decline of partisanship in the future. One is the increasing attachment of individuals to political organizations that serve as practical alternatives to political parties for some. For individuals that have limited their political interests to one or two issues, there may be a perception that single–issue interest groups are a satisfactory alternative to the political party. The individual who opposes abortions, for example, can participate in politics and influence policy making by working through a group such as Right–to–Life. Or an indignant taxpayer seeking tax relief can work through a taxpayers association. Of course, groups like these have always been around as an alternative to parties and have not yet significantly eroded partisanship. But this could change as a more sophisticated use of communications techniques allows interest groups to approach voters directly in greater numbers than ever before. Whatever happens in this regard, however, there will always be roles for parties to play, such as candidate recruitment; but parties may lose their hold over many of their followers.

Interest groups will not be the only groups to use the media to undermine partisan control over voters. We expect that political candidates will continue to use the essentially nonpartisan new–style politics of media–dominated campaigns to woo voters. If this occurs, and if the political parties do not become willing participants in the new technologies of campaigns (some signs suggest they will become involved), the political consultants and other power brokers outside the parties will become dominant forces in electoral behavior. And most of these new political operatives eschew partisanship in their appeals, preferring instead to stress issues or candidate images in their campaign communications. And candidates eager to woo voters away from the other party are willing participants to the strategy of taking partisan appeals out of their campaigns.

In conclusion, several trends suggest that partisanship may hold little if any appeal for voters twenty to thirty years from today. Partisanship, however, is a habit that the electorate seems to find hard to give up. There have been many predictions of the demise of partisanship before; and many of the forces we see undermining partisanship in the future have been present for some time in the past. Thus, we should not be surprised if partisanship proves to be a tenacious survivor in the evolution of American electoral behavior.

Political Participation in the Future

Predicting trends in political participation may be the most difficult task we face in looking to the future. This difficulty is illustrated by the puzzling downward trend in voter turnout during the past two decades. In 1960, if we had predicted that the education of the electorate would be doubled by 1980, we would also have predicted a rise in electoral participation. Well, 1980 has come and so has a doubling of Americans' exposure to higher education; but despite this increase in the educational accomplishment of the electorate, turnout has dropped. We have also eliminated many legal restrictions that prevented some from voting. Nevertheless, turnout has fallen with each successive presidential election. In short, we have some difficulty explaining why people vote or do not vote today. And, perhaps as a consequence of that failure, we cannot successfully explain why people are less likely to vote now than they were in the 1960s. Thus, it should not be surprising that we are not optimistic about our abilities to predict trends in political participation.

One factor which might well contribute to higher participation in future elections (or at least retard further declines in turnout) is the aging of the baby boom cohort. As we noted in Chapter 3, there is a life–cycle effect in voting which causes turnout to increase with age up to about sixty-five years of age. After that age turnout generally decreases, especially among the elderly that live alone, without social reinforcement to vote. If turnout does increase with the aging of the baby boom cohort, then we might also expect it to decline later, approximately thirty-five to forty-five years from now when that cohort is very elderly.

It also seems likely that election laws and procedures will be further relaxed in hope of encouraging participation. Such reforms may be accompanied by technological advances, such as two–way cable television, microcomputer networks, and 900 number DIAL–IT telephone surveys, which make voting and other acts of political participation easier. These advances could open the way for more frequent polling of citizen opinion, or even more frequent use of binding referendums, in making public policies.

There are already signs of such innovations. In April, 1981, San Diego held a ballot referendum by mail on a proposed $224 million bond issue earmarked for construction of a convention complex in the city's downtown area. Each registered voter in the city was sent a ballot which he or she had to return within two weeks from the date the ballots were mailed. The result was a turnout of 61.7 percent of registered voters, a much higher figure than is typical for bond issues where voters must go to a polling place on a single election day in the traditional manner. Oregon is also experimenting with balloting by mail.

AT&T has experimented with a system for straw polls using ordinary telephones—thus leading some to coin the term "teledemocracy." One test of this system came after a nationally televised debate between Jimmy Carter and Ronald Reagan during the 1980 presidential campaign. ABC television asked viewers of the debate to call a special 900 DIAL–IT (the system's proprietary name) number, for which callers were billed fifty cents, to register their opinions about the debate winner. A total of 652,820 voters phoned during the one hour and forty minutes that the telephone lines were open. About two–thirds of the callers declared Ronald Reagan the debate winner. Although those calling represented only a fraction of the forty million people estimated to be watching ABC at the time, and although the opinions of callers were probably not an accurate representation of all viewers, the event was successful in demonstrating the fast–developing technology for citizen input and participation.

Another controversial system of this genre, currently being developed by the Warner–Amex Corporation, is known as "Qube." Qube allows Warner–Amex cable television subscribers in Columbus, Ohio and other cities across the nation to cast votes on various public affairs questions. The system uses two–way interactive cable systems to transmit the audience responses to a central computer which tabulates and displays the results in about ten seconds. Cable advocates predict that this type of technology will be available to most Americans in the not–too–distant future.

Obviously, these presently available technologies offer the possibility of making political participation easier than ever before. Some refinements are necessary, of course, before such innovations can be used for actual referenda. For example, we must be sure that only qualified adult voters are using the voting devices and that multiple voting is not taking place. These problems can and will be solved, however; and once this is accomplished, teledemocracy and its variants may become the mechanism to increase political participation. Proponents of teledemocracy already are vocal. One such advocate, political scientist Ted Becker, predicts that "with the help of teledemocratic processes, public opinion will become the law of the land...."[1] Commenting on initial reactions to Qube, Becker observes that "folks truly enjoy using this teledemocratic system: they express avid interest in participating in feedback; they find the use of the system rewarding. And they are willing to pay for the service." Considering that people often do not use "free" ballots for important elections conducted these days, it is somewhat interesting that they will pay to express their opinions in nonbinding straw polls. The current wave of enthusiasm for Qube, 900 DIAL–IT, and other innovations may not last however. It may be that people are initially drawn to these alternatives because of their novelty value. Many Americans love new things, things that seem different and innovative. But after a while, the new wears off and interest wanes. Declines in interest in new forms of voting will probably soon wipe out any initial increases they make in the rate of political participation.

Political Trust in the Future

Political trust, which in less than two decades has dropped to levels that some observers consider dangerous, will probably not change significantly in the next several years. If anything, political alienation could worsen, but given that most indicators of trust and alienation are already near their worst point, we anticipate that we will see these measures improve somewhat or stabilize at the present level at which most of them have been for three or four years. Already we noted some upturns in political trust after the 1980 election.

Several factors seem to rule out a major rebound in political trust. (We refer to a long–term increase, not simply an increase in political trust that typically occurs for a year or so when a new president is elected.) First, we are unquestionably entering an era in which we will confront a variety of problems—social, economic, and technical—which will defy easy solution, or solution at all. We anticipate that the electorate will become increasingly frustrated with the impotence of government to resolve such problems, thus maintaining low levels of political trust. Second, modern medicine is going to keep more Americans living longer lives than ever before. This should become most significant when the large baby boom cohort reaches its sixties, seventies, and beyond. If the elderly, as in the past, continue to be the most profoundly alienated and distrusting segment of society, and if the elderly make up an increasingly greater percentage of society, then we can only expect higher levels (or at least stable levels) of political distrust. One issue in particular may stimulate this trend. As more and more politicians speak publicly of the necessity of reforming the Social Security system, the elderly that depend on benefits of the program may become increasingly cynical about efforts to cut their monthly pension checks. Third, nothing short of an unprecedented era of national economic prosperity seems likely to cause a dramatic upturn in public confidence. The prospects for this scenario seem poor, however, because almost no economists expect the U.S. economy to ever dominate the world again as it did immediately after World War II, creating a generally booming economy during the 1950s and 1960s. America's dominance of the automobile, steel, and other durable-goods industries will probably never occur again, thus leaving many Americans out of work or underemployed. This trend must unquestionably dampen the American spirit.

What is the long-term impact of political alienation? As we noted in Chapter 4, some theorists have suggested that sustained periods of political alienation could spill over into political violence against the system and leadership. Will this happen in the United States? We think not, because no matter how low public confidence has fallen in recent polls, Americans still profess belief that our system of government is best. Sentiment that the system is in need of major overhaul scarcely can be found in public opinion polls. Although President Carter argued in his now-famous 1979 "malaise" speech that "the erosion of our confidence in the future is threatening to destroy the social and the political fabric of America,"[2] no systematic proof can be found for his position. The key to this matter seems to be found in Americans' perceptions of their personal plight. While most citizens are convinced that political institutions have failed the test of confidence, they nevertheless express considerable satisfaction with their personal and family situations, as Everett Carll Ladd has recently observed.[3] Unless there is some undesirable change in the private situations of most Americans, they are likely to remain loyal to the nation and its system of government. As Daniel Yankelovich concludes, personal satisfaction and optimism will sustain political stability and *"ressentiment* will be kept at bay."[4] Thus the key to political stability becomes the social and economic well-being of the nation rather than the perceived performance of its leadership.

NOTES

1. Becker quoted in Michael Malbin, "Teledemocracy and Its Discontents," *Public Opinion,* 5 (June/July 1982): 58.
2. Congressional Quarterly, *President Carter, 1979* (Washington: Congressional Quarterly, 1980), p. 46-A.
3. Everett Carll Ladd, "205 and Going Strong," *Public Opinion,* 4 (June/July 1981): 7–12.
4. Daniel Yankelovich, "The Status of Ressentiment in America," *Social Research* 42 (Winter 1975): 760–777.

Index